Faye!
My sister!
Thank you for your prayers and support! May the words in this book bring you encouragement.
-Patricia D. Malone

INFLUENCE

365

INFLUENCE

365

Visionary Author

Dr. Derashay Zorn, Kingdom Strategist

For information about special discounts for bulk purchase, contact the sales department at **sales@dormpublishing.com**

Designed by D' Technology

Published by:

D.O.R.M. International Publishing

A Christian Publisher located in Atlanta, Georgia (USA)

Visit our website at **www.dormpublishing.com**

Printed in the United States of America

First Edition: February 2022

10 9 8 7 6 5 4 3 2 1

Library of Congress Cataloging-in-Publication Data

Dr. Derashay Worthen-Zorn

Influence 365 / Dr. Derashay Worthen-Zorn – 1st ed.

ISBN-13: 978-1-957038-01-8

ISBN-10: 1-957038-01-2

DEDICATION

This book is dedicated to every person in the world because we know that God has created you to impact and positively influence the lives of others. It doesn't matter what you have been through in life it all can be used to bring glorification to God. By birthright, you are designed to be an influencer. Through this project, we stand with you to break every stereotype that has been placed upon you, which has formed a false identity. Collectively, we rise as soldiers in the body of Christ in purpose, power, permission, prosperity. We know you are called to impact nations, and we couldn't setback another second without seeing you placed in your rightful position. We are calling forth the influencer within you.

You shall Influence Nations
You shall no longer be hidden
You shall light up the world
You shall do good works for the Kingdom of God
You shall lead others in the way of the Lord
You shall be a leader to your generation
You shall raise up other leaders within your sphere of Influence
Your light shall shine before man
Your gifts shall not be overlooked
Your gifts shall make room for you
Nations shall call upon your name
Your name shall be made great
God shall be glorified through your good works

Influencer Arise & Impact Nations

Get Your Free Resources

A comprehensive package of exclusive resources come with this book as a free bonus. There's also a free online course designed to provide additional guidance. To be sure you get the most out of this book, download all the extras and access the companion course at the link below:

http://bit.ly/Influence365extra

Table of Contents

ACKNOWLEDGMENTS

I want to first give honor and thanks to God for trusting me with this book and every project associated with it. It has been such an honor to have my steps ordered by you.

I want to express gratitude to my co-authors who caught the vision and ran with it. Your collaboration with this project made it unique and just what God ordered for His people. For such a time as this, your light is helping nations to shine. Each of your portions are vital to this journey so that God emerging influencers can have a tool to help them stand up and shine in this dark world. You are special in the sight of God, and He is going to take you to great places. May He continue to expand your borders.

I want to thank Denise Walker, founder and editor in chief of Armor of Hope Writing Services, for your commitment to making this project shine with a spirit of excellence.

I honor my family and friends who support my endeavors. I couldn't do it without you. I would also like to express thanks to every individual who purchases this book. To our readers, know that this book was created with you in mind, and there's something on every page you can use within 365 days a year to guide you in emerging in your influential abilities, wherever God graces your feet. You are bringing it to life. We declare you will no longer be hidden or go unnoticed because you are the city on the hill that cannot be hidden.

INFLUENCE
365

Visionary Author

Dr. Derashay Zorn, Kingdom Strategist

INTRODUCTION

As I looked at what was happening around the world and so many people consumed with the loss of loved ones, the rise of injustice, hopelessness within the land, and wickedness running rampant, I knew there was a solution to transform what was happening around the world. So that peace and hope can be restored in people's lives in all nations. Pondering for a solution, the scripture Mathew 5:14-16 came to my heart and as I began to meditate on it, I knew it was the answer to what is needed for change within this dark and cold world. This world needs the light of Jesus Christ to illuminate through it consistently. And God desires to use people like you and me to be the light of the world to lead others out of darkness into the marvelous light.

Therefore, Influence 365 was birth to provide individuals with a tool that they can use 365 days a year, 24 hours a day, and 7 days a week for the purpose of obtaining the substance they need to be the light in whatever environment they are in. So that lives can be changed as they walk as the light and help others become the light of the world. We live in a dark world that is consuming people with depression, suicide, and all type of evil and wickedness. There is hope and Jesus Christ is the answer. But how would they know if there's no one there to teach them Him, show them the way, and be an example before them?

This devotion serves as a tool to encourage, equip, educate, employ others to live a life that positively impacts and changes themselves, others, and their environment so that God can be glorified. It is composed of words of affirmations, motivation, inspiration, prayers, poems, and action steps to bring strength, hope, and encouragement to bring out the influencers within its reader.

This project is based on Matthew 5:14-16

"You are the light of the world. A city that is set on a hill cannot be hidden. Nor do they light a lamp and put it under a basket, but on a lampstand, and it gives light to all who are in the house. Let your light so shine before men, that they may see your good works and glorify your Father in heaven. "

CLAIM YOUR THRONE!!!!

Dr. Derashay Zorn, Kingdom Strategist

"Now Solomon the son of David was strengthened in his kingdom, and the Lord his God was with him and exalted him exceedingly."

2 Chronicles 1:1 NKJV

It's time to take ownership and possession of that in which God has entrusted to us. We can no longer afford to operate our kingdoms under the shadow or in duplication of others. Be authentically you!!! This is your key to establishing a solid reign within your business industry. What it takes to successfully run someone else's empire may not be the requirements to run yours, so be clear on what it takes to effectively run what God has given to you. When King Solomon took over the throne in the book of Chronicles, we saw how quickly he made the necessary adjustments to fortify his kingdom so he could rule effectively. There were defining things that King Solomon knew needed to take place so his rulership would be established. He couldn't follow his father's pattern. He had to come into what God had chosen for him. When you rule authentically, God will give you everything you tread upon, and your work will be established.

Entrepreneur Thought: Are there any adjustments you need to make in your endeavors to accomplish what God has called you to do? Do you need to stop copying others and seek God for how you should operate your business or ministry?

Entrepreneur Prayer: *Father, I thank you for entrusting me to reign in my gifts and talents so you can be glorified. Give me the wisdom to never alter what you have designed to make others comfortable, in Jesus' name, amen.*

REFLECTION:

____

____

____

____

____

____

Kingdom Strategist, Blueprint Builder, and Spiritual Midwife, Dr. Derashay Zorn is an international business coach and best-selling author. She helps the faith-based community magnetize and monetize their influence and impact by creating profitable brands that develop long-lasting relationships with products and services their ideal client loves.

Discover how she can take your message and develop your next book, membership program, course, educational platform, coaching program, and more by visiting https://px.fyi/teawiththestrategist.

Social Media FB | IG: kingdom.strategist **Website:** www.derashay.com

OUR YEAR OF JUBILEE

Dr. Rolanda S. Watson

"And so, it is written, the first man Adam became a living soul. The last man Adam became a life-giving Spirit"

1 Cor. 15:45

A soul must receive life to live. A spirit gives life so others may live. What the first man, Adam, lost; the last man, Adam (Jesus), begot in restoration.
Restoration is the very essence of "The Year of Jubilee"

Jubilee literally means "ram" or "ram's horn". In one instance, it is declared "trumpet". The term is associated with the year of Jubilee in Leviticus 25:10 and Numbers 36:4. The fiftieth year was "jubilee" the year for the Hebrews, marked by the blowing of the trumpet.
During this year, the Israelites experienced freedom and liberty. Slaves were freed, debts were cancelled, the land was left fallow, and family property was redeemed. The fact that Jesus quoted Is 48:8-10, strongly indicates that He equated His earthly ministry with the principles regarding the Year of Jubilee. According to Luke 4: 14-19, this is the year of Jubilee! The devil doesn't want us to know this and the televangelist only preached Jubilee for a season. The church is in its season of Jubilee. It's not over. Now, celebrate and give God the Glory that is due His name! We, the saints, must recognize our Jubilee because the manifestation of Jubilee is only when we recognize it. Recognizing Jubilee is the prerequisite for partaking of it. Blessings in Jesus' name!

REFLECTION:

Dr. Watson is an international best-selling author, certified life coach, and entrepreneur. Residing in Atlanta, she is committed to empowering women in the areas of business and ministry.

Social Media: FB: Rolanda S. Watson **IG:** @Rolandaswatson

YOUR GLORY SURROUNDS ME

Dr. Dawn L. Cooper

"one cluster of grapes…bare it between two"

Num. 13:23

Have you ever been awestruck in seeing the glory of God? Perhaps it was in a vibrant rainbow, the luminous red glow from a setting sun, or maybe the varying hues of green and blue along an ocean shore. Whatever it was, it caused you to stop in your tracks and take notice.

Joshua and Caleb experienced this when they entered the promised land. They saw clusters of grapes so big it took two men to carry it or when Moses and his people witnessed God splitting the Red Sea.

Sometimes we have things that leave us captivated, yet God's glory is all around us. Every day I open the blinds to my prayer room and see the tops of trees from my second floor and the little hand of my granddaughter as she places it in mine. I stop in wander of how God made us and trees dependent upon one another and how He placed everything in my granddaughter at birth that she needed to grow into an adult. That is God's glory.

Today, stop and reflect on God's glory around you. Don't take it for granted.

REFLECTION:

Dr. Dawn L. Cooper is an international best-selling author who resides in Indianapolis, Indiana. She is called by God to deliver biblical principles that build the Kingdom of God on Earth. Dr. Cooper is the mother of six and the grandmother of 12.

Social Media FB: @dlcooperauthor **Website:** https://dlcooperauthor.com

SUSTAINING THE ANOINTING

Nico Olivia

"And let us consider how to stir up one another to love and good works."

Heb. 10:24 (ESV)

The Anointing does not sustain you!

It is your relationship with the God-head and the interweaving of His Word, prayer, fasting, worship and obedience to God that sustains the Anointing in You!

Your character should be imbedded in your relationship with God!

You possess an anointing that's distinct to you! To everything there is a time and season in the earth. Whilst the Lord is establishing you as you do your part in relationship building with Him, learn to clap for your brothers and sisters and continue clapping. Celebrate others!

Say a kind word of encouragement and affirmation that will propel them forward and keep them motivated. The Word of God says that we should stir each other up to love and good works!

Covid-19 has certainly hampered our ability to meet in a conventional sense at the moment, BUT we are meeting each other and crossing paths in the digital arena. With a genuine spirit, like, react, share, comment, connect, build, and encourage one another. Let it be a lifelong practice of stoking the flames of each other's spirit and passion for the Kingdom and life.

REFLECTION:

Nico Olivia is the founder and creative director of multimedia and brand communication company - Eminence. Her expertise includes copywriting and marketing strategist for companies in the Marketing and Advertising industry.

As a Kingdom scribe who carries an Apostolic Prophetic / Intercessory mantle, she specializes in counselling, coaching, business coaching, business administration, training, self-development, and personal mastery, both in the Kingdom and secular environment.

Social Media FB: nico.o.favour | **IG:** iam_nicoolivia

OBEY GOD

Sharon P. Jones

"But if thou shalt indeed obey his voice and do all that I speak; then I will be an enemy unto thine enemies, and an adversary unto thine adversaries

Exodus 23:32

"But if thou shalt indeed obey his voice and do all that I speak; then I will be an enemy unto thine enemies, and an adversary unto thine adversaries (Exodus 23:22)." Obedience, according to Merriam-Webster, means compliance with an order, request, or law or submission to another's authority. God has us on His mind. He knew us before we were formed in our mother's womb. God loves us so much and has our best interest at heart.

Knowing this about God, we should obey Him. We always seek Him for answers. Therefore, we should obey Him with the instructions He provides. We must obey God with our ears and keep Him as our first love. We must love God more than anything. The troubles we face come from disobedience and lack of faith. Let's commit to submit ourselves completely to God. Study the holy scriptures, and let God be God.

"Then shalt thou enquire, and make search, and ask diligently; and behold, if it be truth, and the thing certain, that such abomination is wrought among you (Deuteronomy 13:4)."

REFLECTION:

Sharon P. Jones is an international best-selling author, certified life coach and entrepreneur. She is a wife and mother who lives in Atlanta where she serves in ministry with her husband.

Social Media FB | IG: @wotflglobal**; Facebook:** Sharon Jones Author

ATTACK, RESCUE, & CONQUER

Dr. Cecilia Jackson

"I will go and fight him." David said, "I take care of my father's sheep. Any time a lion or a bear carries off a lamb, I go after it, attack it, and rescue the lamb"

1Sa 17:32-35 (GNB).

David said anytime a lion or bear would carry away his father's sheep, he would make an offensive and aggressive move. He would go after the intruder, attack it, and rescue the lamb. If the lion or bear turned on him, he would grab it by the throat and beat it to death. Grabbing by the throat means to enact control, weaken, and defeat. Everything about David's actions was offensive, even to the point of destroying the enemy.

Any time the enemy TRIES to take something from you, or if he has taken anything, offensively and aggressively take it back. Realize the enemy is already destroyed by the power and blood of Christ. God's word states your strength, happiness, safety, family, confidence, dreams, and hope, are guaranteed a successful end (Jer. 29:11).

Attack and rescue with your offensive weapons of salvation, praise, worship, the Word of God, prayer, faith, truth, righteousness, the angelic hosts, and the fruit of the spirit.

David's intense approach of moving offensively and destroying the work of the enemy, Goliath, is what propelled him to his greater purpose, his next level on his journey from shepherd to king.

REFLECTION:

____

____

____

____

____

____

____

Dr. Cecilia Jackson is: 1) Official Delegate of the United Nations for the Cause of Women 2) Author of 36 professional publications 3) Founder and Co-Provost of the "I AM" College of Ministry 4) Founder of Seasoned Anointed Oil for Regional Women in Leadership 5) State Certified Educator 6) Radio Show 7) spiritual Mid-wife Email: drcjackson3712@gmail.com

Social Media FB | IG: I AM Productions Publishing

Website: iamfellowshipministries.net

YOU ARE MY PEACE

Nichole Flowers

"keep him in perfect peace whose mind is stayed on him"

Isaiah 26:3

People often say, "God won't place more on you than you can bear, or there is nothing too hard for God." It's not until you are faced with adversity that you realize these words are true.

No one wakes up in the morning prepared for the storms they will face. Some storms are tiny ones while others seem like Hurricane Katrina came plowing through your living room. No matter the size of your storm, God is wanting you to place it in his hands so he can take over. Just as he did it for Peter on the water, he can and will step in to calm you and provide peace so you can make it through your storm.

Today...cast your cares upon him so that he can be the peace you need to make it through this storm.

REFLECTION:

Nichole Flowers is first and foremost a child of God! She operates in the gift of teaching in a public school setting in Indianapolis, Indiana.

She is a school mom to 25 boys and girls and the biological mother of 1 amazing son. She is also a proud member of Alpha Omega Chi Sorority Incorporated.

Social Media FB | nichole.flowers

FREEDOM

Melissa Baines

"He heals the brokenhearted and binds up their wounds"

Psalm 147:3.

God is so good to us. Nothing we can see with our natural eye has to especially happen. Every day is a blessing and sometimes, a miracle. Each day is full of grace, mercy and (should be) considered a blessing. He deserves praise(s) and our trust. Anything less is apathetic, blind, boorish, brash, discourteous, egocentric, heeless, inattentive, indelicate, insensitive, neglectful, negligent, primitive, rash, reckless, rude, self-centered, selfish, uncaring, unceremonious, ungracious, unheeding, unkind, unattractive, unmindful, unrefined, careless, demanding, dissatisfied, faultfinding, forgetful, an ingrate, insensible, oblivious, self-centered, selfish, thankless, unappreciative, unmindful, and unthankful on our part.

Thank You God for your Grace, Mercy and Forgiveness. Humbled.

No punches pulled; the truth will make you free!

REFLECTION:

Melissa, more familiarly known as Missy/Sis. Missy, considers herself as one The Lord is completing His Good Work in. Among her many Kingdom Assignments, her most meaningful and heartwarming are that of an adoptive and God mother, missionary, and exhorter. The Lord uses Missy strategically in diverse relationships and networking, where her faith is shared freely.

Social Media FB | Melissa (Missy) Baines

DESPERATION HAS A SOUND

Temecka Smith

"When Bartimaeus heard that it was Jesus of Nazareth, he began to shout and say, "Jesus, Son of David (Messiah), have mercy on me"

Mark 10:47 AMP.

The story of Blind Bartimaeus reminds us that Jesus truly is the answer to our needs. He is the only one who can save us from our circumstances, our choices, and set us on a new path. It's okay to cry out to him with any issue and situation you have. Jesus wants us to rely and depend on him for everything, rather big or small. I'm reminded of my children and those who are parents. When they want something, they will get your attention if they have to cry out, scream, or beg. Depending on what it is, we answer to their cry. We serve a good, good father who loves when we call upon him. Be encouraged and cultivate your relationship with Jesus. Expectation is the breeding ground for miracles

REFLECTION:

Temecka Smith is an International Best Selling Author, Relationship Coach, Founder of Real Life Real Issues, Associate Pastor of Good Samaritan Center of Hope, and most of all, a servant of the most high God Jesus Christ. She works with individuals personally and corporately through her coaching program to equip and develop them in areas they lack, getting to the root of the issues through counseling courses, and much more. She has a passion for equipping wives and women in waiting with the tools to be all God called them as Mothers, Wives, Business owners, etc.

You can locate me at @temeckasmith/Facebook and Instagram

Social Media FB | IG: @temeckasmith

GIVE BIRTH TO YOUR DESTINY

Dr. Derashay Zorn, Kingdom Strategist

"But we are not of those who draw back to perdition, but of those who believe to the saving of the soul."

Hebrews 10:39 NJKV

We start off our year with goals, dreams, and visions. By the end of the first quarter, we have given up on many of those aspirations. I want to speak endurance today on that in which God has placed in your heart. Don't let your goals, dreams, and visions fade away under any circumstances. God has put it inside of you because He has empowered you to carry out the task to its completion. Don't allow your current situation, condition, or environment to cause you to draw back from what He has placed in your heart. You must continue to run this race by faith, and it will be the substance that will allow you to manifest God's words.

I speak over your life and declare that you will not draw back from your goals, dreams, or visions. You shall not abort the word of the Lord for your life. We rebuke the drawback spirit, in the name of Jesus. We cancel every spiritual abortion trying to take place in your life, in the powerful name of Jesus. We plead the blood of Jesus Christ over your life, every goal, dream and vision God has given unto you, and we declare they shall come forth in the land of the living, in Jesus' name, amen, amen, and amen...

REFLECTION:

Kingdom Strategist, Blueprint Builder, and Spiritual Midwife, Dr. Derashay Zorn is an international business coach and best-selling author. She helps the faith-based community magnetize and monetize their influence and impact by creating profitable brands that develop long-lasting relationships with products and services their ideal client loves.

Discover how she can take your message and develop your next book, membership program, course, educational platform, coaching program, and more by visiting https://px.fyi/teawiththestrategist.

Social Media FB | IG: kingdom.strategist **Website:** www.derashay.com

HALF-FULL OR HALF-EMPTY

Dr. Rolanda S. Watson

"Finally, brethren, whatever things are true… whatever things are of a good report"

Phil. 4:8.

Embracing an attitude of a good report is one principle that entrepreneurs and companies are teaching their employees and upper management to remain on the cutting-edge in business. Of all the principles available, this one is the most important. This key will serve as the foundation in which the others will rest. You can choose to be a person of good report. Keep in mind, what you choose will also be your fate. What you choose is going to determine what happens to you economically. What you choose is going to determine the success or failure of your business. Anybody can focus on the negative, fault-find, talk about, and tear-down. It doesn't take any capacity to be negative; it takes aptitude to be positive during negative circumstances. When you choose to be positive, you lay a foundation that God can build upon. It doesn't matter how bad things are, "even a broken clock is right twice a day." The most important ingredient to a turnaround is choosing what you regard. Becoming a person of a good report will propel you into a new trajectory and dimension. It is a matter of choice. Make a choice to count the good things you've done; specifically, your successes not failures.

REFLECTION:

Dr. Watson is an international best-selling author, certified life coach, and entrepreneur. Residing in Atlanta, she is committed to empowering women in the areas of business and ministry.

Social Media: FB: Rolanda S. Watson **IG:** @Rolandaswatson

ILLUMINATION

Melissa Baines

"You are the light of the world. A town built on a hill cannot be hidden. Neither do people light a lamp and put it under a bowl. Instead, they put it on its stand, and it gives light to everyone in the house. 16 In the same way, let your light shine before others, that they may see your good deeds and glorify your Father in Heaven"
Matthew 5:14-16 NIV.

Has a light in your life gone out? Someone you looked to and sought counsel from or someone whom you loved has transition home to be with the Lord?

Remember, the Lord calls us lights. We all walk a path that requires a "lamp" or illumination. Could it be, He's positioned, prepared, even gifted us with lanterns in this life, whose flicker reminisces? After a while, like a vapor, instantly life can be no more? Don't take anyone for granted. Listen a little harder, a little longer. Make memories that will last long after their light turns to the off position. If you need them to walk such a narrow path, even should you stumble off, it is better to have their beacon or to recall their guidance and gateway, than to end up feeling your own way through a dark, dark world; especially, when tomorrow is already not promised. Still, we have so many more promises in our arsenal.

Where was/is the light of your life leading you? There is where they will always be.

REFLECTION:

____

____

____

____

____

____

____

____

Melissa, more familiarly known as Missy/Sis. Missy, considers herself as one The Lord is completing His Good Work in. Among her many Kingdom Assignments, her most meaningful and heartwarming are that of an adoptive and God mother, missionary, and exhorter. The Lord uses Missy strategically in diverse relationships and networking, where her faith is shared freely.

Social Media FB | Melissa (Missy) Baines

PURPOSE – BE THE BEST YOU!

Dr. Cecilia Jackson, Apostle

"God has saved us and called us, not because of our efforts, but for His purpose, professional choosing, and divine favor given to us in Christ Jesus before the world began"

II Tim. 1:9

The God of eternity's past, present, and future wrote your narrative and thesis that speaks of your life on earth. Each paragraph was skillfully documented before the beginning of earth in chronological order. Furthermore, the Lord Jesus bestowed upon you His divine endorsement and distinguished authority to successfully live every chapter of your life's story. He desires you to trust His guidance concerning what He has scribed for you. You are His élite original; crafted with incomparable ingenuity. It is only fitting that your journey and destination are unique and customized only for you.

Persevere and accomplish all that was written and supernaturally blown into you by the breath of God. You were strategically placed on earth as an ambassador of change for your family, community, and nation, all for the Kingdom of God! Your destiny is secure! No matter how challenging the valley or mountain experience, DO the best you.

REFLECTION:

Dr. Cecilia Jackson is an apostle, prophet, teacher, author of 30+ publications, English professor, former UN delegate, and 40- year veteran Kingdom Lector. (drcjackson3712@gmail.com).

Social Media FB | IG: I AM Productions Publishing

Website: iamfellowshipministries.net

DISCOVER YOUR PASSION

Wakeitha Cunningham

"I will instruct you and teach you in the way you should go."

Psalm 32:8

Are you living or existing?

God does not expect us to be perfect, but he does want us to be whole. If you are just existing, you are doing what you need to do to stay alive. However, if you are living, you are enjoying life and every moment of it! If you are not enjoying life, you are merely existing, and it's time to discover what you are truly passionate about! As a passion pursuer coach, my mission is to help others pursue their passions and their God given calling!

How to discover your passion:

1. Seek God's guidance and DO SOMETHING!
2. Connect with your WHY!
3. Do what brings you joy! What energizes you?
4. Volunteer with organizations that interest you!
5. Start a new hobby!

Focus on your passion(s) instead of your problems and pain. ~ Wakeitha Cunningham

REFLECTION:

___

___

___

___

___

___

___

Wakeitha Cunningham is a passion pursuer coach, international best-selling author, speaker, a mother of two, and an influential woman of God on a mission to be a light to God's people. She has a passion for helping others pursue their passions and walk in their God given purpose. Wakeitha encourages others to focus on their passions instead of their problems and pain.

Email: coachwcunningham@gmail.com

USE THE GIFT

Dr. Derashay Zorn, Kingdom Strategist

"A man's gift makes room for him, And brings him before great men" Proverbs 18:16.

God has given us gifts we must utilize to magnetize and monetize. Joseph had a dream about being a leader, and he was mocked by all in his family. Like many, he had family members who didn't like him, and they wanted to kill him. They ended up selling him as a slave instead. He ended up in prison. There were two people, who worked for the king of Egypt, in destress. Joseph used his gift to help them. The men got out, and his words to them came to pass. One day the king of Egypt was distressed, and his servant remembered Joseph. He told the king about him. The king called for him, and he helped the king, relieving his distress. This very moment brought Joseph's dream to life as he became second in command over Egypt. Had Joseph not utilized his gift while he was in prison to help the men, this wouldn't have happened. If you do not use the gift, it can never make room for you and place you among great men. Gifts are discovered by others when they are seen in action. It's time to move in the gift God has given you so you can walk in the doors He has opened and given you access to great men.

Entrepreneur Thought: Are you authentically utilizing the gift God has given you no matter what the conditions may be?

Entrepreneur Prayer: *Father, give me the wisdom to utilize my gifts for your glorification, and I thank you for where they will take me, in Jesus' name, amen.*

REFLECTION:

____

____

____

____

____

Kingdom Strategist, Blueprint Builder, and Spiritual Midwife, Dr. Derashay Zorn is an international business coach and best-selling author. She helps the faith-based community magnetize and monetize their influence and impact by creating profitable brands that develop long-lasting relationships with products and services their ideal client loves.

Discover how she can take your message and develop your next book, membership program, course, educational platform, coaching program, and more by visiting https://px.fyi/teawiththestrategist.

Social Media FB | IG: kingdom.strategist **Website:** www.derashay.com

LIVE BY FAITH

Sandra Howell

"For we live by faith, not by sight"

2 Cor.5:7.

During certain moments of your journey, you will encounter moments of confusion. The road ahead seems dark and uncertain. Walking through darkness can be scary, especially when you can't see where you're going. You may even feel alone. During those times, you have to TRUST because you've gotta faith walk it the rest of the way. Be encouraged and always allow GOD to direct your path. With him leading the way, you can achieve beyond anything you ever imagined or dreamed. Know that the enemy can't try you without God allowing it. With that being said, while your being tested, God is evaluating your performance! Remember, He wants to measure your faith and see your work. Despite the obstacles, know His plans are greater, and your breakthrough is linked to what you've been through!

REFLECTION:

Sandra Howell is a mother, friend, and mentor with a strong passion for outreach. Her love brings healing to people who have been through a traumatic/stressful experience. She helps individuals find healthy perceptions of themselves and strengthen their relationships so they can know themselves as peaceful, complete, whole, and safe. Her favorite scripture is Psalms 91. When she is not helping others, she enjoys cooking.

Social Media FB | IG: Sandra Howell

GOD INTENDED

Melissa Baines

And the same John had his raiment of camel's hair, and a leathern girdle about his loins; and his meat was locusts and wild honey.

Matthew 3:4

While praying that Lord would bring each of my children into their purposes, that the path they each walk, brings them straight into their Kingdom purpose, Matthew 3:4 came to mind, "John's clothes were made of camel's hair, and he had a leather belt around his waist. His food was locusts and wild honey." I was reminded that John the Baptist was considered strange by most but was respected as a mighty man of God by many. It was revealed to me that perhaps Zachariah and Elizabeth were a bit disappointed in not only his appearance but in his apparent way of life - living in the wilderness, when they had brought him up decently, and dressing in a substandard way and eating like the homeless. Yet, they understood and stood on the Word they'd received over his life, and he fulfilled it, even to the point of death. This is something any parent would protest over their child). The good thing is he ended up in the father's will and presence, and that's all that matters.

I hope this brings some solace and hope, as it did me.

REFLECTION:

Melissa, more familiarly known as Missy/Sis. Missy, considers herself as one The Lord is completing His Good Work in. Among her many Kingdom Assignments, her most meaningful and heartwarming are that of adoptive and god mother, Missionary and exhorter. The Lord uses Missy strategically in diverse relationships and networking, where her faith is shared freely.

Social Media FB | Melissa (Missy) Baines

LEFT OUT, BUT NOT FORGOTTEN

Sharon Dawson-McElveen

"And Samuel said unto Jesse, Are here all thy children? And he said, There remaineth yet the youngest, and, behold, he keepeth the sheep. And Samuel said unto Jesse, Send and fetch him: for we will not sit down till he come hither. And he sent, and brought him in. Now he was ruddy, and withal of a beautiful countenance, and goodly to look to. And the Lord said, Arise, anoint him: for this is he."

1 Samuel 16:11-12

As a child, I yearned for the attention and affirmations from my mother. Not that she did not love me or take care of me, but as the middle child in my family, there was an older brother and a younger sister who received a different kind of attention

There were times when I felt alone and wanted to isolate. These were times I would take comfort in Jesus. Although I was not able to participate in the majority of the fun activities, it made me feel left out. Today, you might feel left out and overlooked, but that does not mean you are forgotten. Jessie called seven of his sons who he considered to be worthy of the calling. However, God had other plans. Just as He has called David as His chosen vessel, you have been chosen too. God is not looking for popularity, intellect, nor is He concerned about your appearance. He sees the matters of your heart. Little did I know as a child I would be the chosen one. As the oil was being poured onto David's head, the oil is graced to be poured for you and me. Although there may be times when you feel left out, just know, you are not forgotten.

REFLECTION:.

____

____

____

____

____

____

____

Born and raised in New York City, Sharon felt a calling on her life as a young girl. Pastor Sharon holds a master's degree in Pastoral Care and Christian Counseling. She is the founder of Rose of Sharon Street Outreach Ministries, LLC. She serves as the Pastor over the outreach ministries at her church, where she leads her team in serving the community and those under bridges.

Social Media FB: Sharon Dawson McElveen

CATCH YOUR VISION

Dr. Derashay Zorn, Kingdom Strategist

"Where there is no revelation, the people cast off restraint; But happy is he who keeps the law."

Prov. 29:18 NKJV

Vision is essential to the success of any endeavor. It gives site as it brings an individual, business, or organization to a specific point of focus. Therefore, maximize your resources and efforts as you utilize them to meet your particular target. Without vision, you are wasting time, resources, and efforts because you are operating aimlessly. Visionless actions have caused many to abort what they desired to do because they did not yield fruitful results.

Assignment:

1. Define your target.
2. Create actions steps to hit your target.
3. Follow the plan.

Entrepreneur Thought: Do your activities line up with the vision that God has given you? If not, make necessary adjustments.

Entrepreneur Prayer: *Dear God, I thank you for the vision you have given me. Remove everything that has me off track from moving in your word so it shall not come back void, in Jesus' name, amen.*

REFLECTION:

____

____

____

____

____

____

____

Kingdom Strategist, Blueprint Builder, and Spiritual Midwife, Dr. Derashay Zorn is an international business coach and best-selling author. She helps the faith-based community magnetize and monetize their influence and impact by creating profitable brands that develop long-lasting relationships with products and services their ideal client loves.

Discover how she can take your message and develop your next book, membership program, course, educational platform, coaching program, and more by visiting https://px.fyi/teawiththestrategist.

Social Media FB | IG: kingdom.strategist **Website:** www.derashay.com

TRIAL BY FIRE

Sharon P. Jones

"That the trial of your faith, being much more precious than of gold that perisheth, though he tried with fire, might be found unto praise and honour and glory at the appearing of Jesus Christ:"

1 Peter 1:7

Trial by fire means a test of one's abilities to perform well under pressure.

In the process of trial by fire, there is pressure, pain, and discomfort. Sometimes there is emotional pain in the trial by fire. While in the fire, it is important to remain focused. One must be intentional to be steadfast and unmovable. This simply means to stand firm and maintain position while in the process and do not waver. Also, maintain love in your heart, joy, prayer, and devotional time. Commit to this daily. The book of James 1:12 reminds us, "Blessed is the man that endureth temptation: for when he is tried, he shall receive the crown of life, which the Lord hath promised to them that love him." Allow yourself to trust God in this purification process.

REFLECTION:

Sharon P. Jones is an international best-selling author, certified life coach and entrepreneur. She is a wife and mother who lives in Atlanta where she serves in ministry with her husband.

Social Media FB | IG: @wotflglobal; **Facebook:** Sharon Jones Author

PRAYER AGAINST BARRENNESS

Dr. Derashay Zorn, Kingdom Strategist

"Now Isaac pleaded with the LORD for his wife because she was barren; and the LORD granted his plea, and Rebekah, his wife, conceived"

Genesis 25:21 NKJV

In the name of Jesus, we declare your places of barrenness have just become fertile. We decree there will be no more barrenness in your ministry, marriage, finances, relationships, business, health, career, or education. You shall conceive and bring forth the richness of the Lord in every area of your life. In the mighty name of Jesus. Amen

REFLECTION:

Kingdom Strategist, Blueprint Builder, and Spiritual Midwife, Dr. Derashay Zorn is an international business coach and best-selling author. She helps the faith-based community magnetize and monetize their influence and impact by creating profitable brands that develop long-lasting relationships with products and services their ideal client loves.

Discover how she can take your message and develop your next book, membership program, course, educational platform, coaching program, and more by visiting https://px.fyi/teawiththestrategist.

Social Media FB | IG: kingdom.strategist **Website:** www.derashay.com

EMBRACE THE SHIFT!

Dr. Derashay Zorn, Kingdom Strategist

"Do not remember the former things, Nor consider the things of old. Behold, I will do a new thing, Now it shall spring forth; Shall you not know it? I will even make a road in the wilderness And rivers in the desert."

Isa. 43:18-19 NKJV

God is shifting things in the earth, and many are being very resistant to the shift. Don't try to keep holding on to familiar things when God is trying to do something new in your life. Don't allow the way of old to hinder you from stepping into the new in Christ Jesus. The former things cannot even compare to what is to come. You have cried, prayed, and fasted for the very thing you are resisting. Just because God is sending it in a different way than which you were expecting it, uncertainty is trying to hinder you.

He cannot take you to a place you are resisting to go because your resistance will cause you to faint on your journey. It's time to embrace the shift so you can move forward in that which has been tarring.

You cannot move forward holding on to what's behind you!

Dear God, I thank you for my ability to embrace the new things you have planned for me, in Jesus' name, amen.

REFLECTION:

____

____

____

____

____

____

____

____

Kingdom Strategist, Blueprint Builder, and Spiritual Midwife, Dr. Derashay Zorn is an international business coach and best-selling author. She helps the faith-based community magnetize and monetize their influence and impact by creating profitable brands that develop long-lasting relationships with products and services their ideal client loves.

Discover how she can take your message and develop your next book, membership program, course, educational platform, coaching program, and more by visiting https://px.fyi/teawiththestrategist.

Social Media FB | IG: kingdom.strategist **Website:** www.derashay.com

GRANDMOTHER'S PRAYERS: THE LORD IS MY SHEPHERD

Sharon Dawson-McElveen

"The Lord is my Shepherd. I shall not want. He makes me lie down in green pastures. He leads me beside the still waters."

Psalm 23:1-6

My sweet grandmother, Mollie, loved the 23rd Psalm. She was graced, beautiful, and a woman of virtue. She made her own clothes and grew her garden. She baked from scratch and made a home of comfort and love for her family. Most of all, she loved the Lord. During her times in prayer, she always took comfort as she prayed, in times of good or bad, "The Lord is my Shepherd."

When King David was going through a dark and perilous times, he prayed, and we can pattern ourselves by his prayers by being restored and led into the Father's will.

If you ever find you are going through a period of turbulence or maybe a time of joy, you can pray the 23rd Psalm and know that the Lord is your Shephard. He goes before us and guides us to ensure our purpose and destiny. He fights on our behalf and blesses us with his goodness.

Just like my grandmother, when you don't know where to turn or begin, you can always find comfort and restoration, as you receive healing and protection. Take refuge, for your Shephard is with you always.

REFLECTION:

____

____

____

____

____

____

____

Born and raised in New York City, Sharon felt a calling on her life as a young girl. Pastor Sharon holds a master's degree in Pastoral Care and Christian Counseling. She is the founder of Rose of Sharon Street Outreach Ministries, LLC. She serves as the Pastor over the outreach ministries at her church, where she leads her team in serving the community and those under bridges.

Social Media FB: Sharon Dawson McElveen

A TALK WITH NANA

Evangelist Vickie Chiney-Smith

"Not that I speak in respect of want: for I have learned, in whatsoever state I am, therewith to be content "

Philippians 4:11.

One day, a grandmother was chatting with her adult granddaughter, "Nana, do you think we find answers or just adapt and become content?" Good question! Much like this granddaughter, we may be curious about the same thing. First of all, we are comprised of three things: body, mind, and soul. The body is flesh. It is never content and has a short attention span! It goes along with the trend or status quo. The mind makes choices and tells the body what to do, according to what feels good. It is born with innate sinful behavior, which comes naturally throughout life. The soul or nature of a human is the spirit. The spirit does not just adapt! It searches for moral meaning, connects to it, and follows it. The mind chooses what it does based on what it identifies with; the flesh-man or the spirit-man.

The two operate opposite each other. First, we are all born in the spirit of the flesh (Satan), which is evil (innate behavior); it seeks and serves sinful pleasure. Secondly, the Spirit of God is moral; it seeks and serves God's righteousness. To even know what God wants, you must be born again and regenerated. You will no longer operate in the flesh but in the Spirit of God. You will seek Jesus for all answers and what pleases God (learned behavior). Your true nature determines what you follow! As far as contentment, like Paul, we learn how to be content. The Holy Ghost teaches and strengthens us through Christ. Don't just adapt; seek God's will in your life, and you will be content.

REFLECTION:

____

____

____

____

____

____

____

____

Evangelist Vickie Chiney-Smith (EVCS) is a servant of God, dedicated to Kingdom building. She hosts the MID-DAY weekly Bible Study every Tuesday @ 2pm CST on Divine Order Restoration Ministries FB, Dr. Derashay Zorn, Kingdom Strategist, founder. EVCS goes by "The Praise Raiser." Her motto is: "RAISE THE PRAISE (RTP)! ALRIGHT!

Social Media FB: RTPEVCS **Website:** http://www.thepraiseraiser.com

KEEP THE FAITH

Dr. Derashay Zorn, Kingdom Strategist

"I have fought the good fight, I have finished the race, I have kept the faith. "

2 Timothy 4:7 NKJV

Every entrepreneur faces challenges within the course of starting and running a business. These challenges can sometimes bring discouragement, fear, and frustration that can cause you to want to give up. Many people never get to see the fullness of God's promise because this is where they throw in the towel. I want to encourage you to keep the faith in these defining moments in your entrepreneurial endeavor. It is your faith that will give you the fuel to continue to move forward in times of adversity. Actually, what you truly believe in will be the determining factor of you quitting the race or completing it. When you believe in something, you don't mind fighting for it. You have heard that anything worth having is worth fighting for. This should hold true for the promises of God for your life. When opposition comes, you can remind yourself of God's promise, read His word, pray, or call your accountability team for support. One of my favorite things to do is to measure the circumstances against the word of God, and it never fails to expose a counterfeit situation.

Entrepreneur Thought: What strategies do you use when times get hard?

Entrepreneur Prayer: *Father, I thank you for the strategy to keep my faith through trying times so I may overcome my enemies, in Jesus' name, amen.*

REFLECTION:

Kingdom Strategist, Blueprint Builder, and Spiritual Midwife, Dr. Derashay Zorn is an international business coach and best-selling author. She helps the faith-based community magnetize and monetize their influence and impact by creating profitable brands that develop long-lasting relationships with products and services their ideal client loves.

Discover how she can take your message and develop your next book, membership program, course, educational platform, coaching program, and more by visiting https://px.fyi/teawiththestrategist.

Social Media FB | IG: kingdom.strategist **Website:** www.derashay.com

CAPITULATED GRATITUDE

Milagros Romero

"In all things give thanks: for this is the will of God…"

1 Thess. 5:18.

Have you ever been through something so horrible you found no reason to be grateful? There was a time when I was lost within the darkness of a devastation that swallowed me whole. Gratitude was the furthest thing from my mind. My soul only desired death. I knew God was with me as I walked through a valley, which I felt only offered me a living hell. I was barricaded by pain and could not see nor feel His love. I was nothing. I had nothing and felt nothing. How then could I feel gratitude? How would I recognize anything good or even a sign of kindness when brokenness was my daily bread? I simply could not. However, God was with me through every step, and His grace, mercy, and love rescued me. He set me free, and my soul began to see the power of the blessings and the degree of the gift in my life that could only come from what I endured. Appreciation then flourished within me, and now I live in capitulated gratitude.

Allow gratitude to become the place where your praises meet God's favor. A grateful heart blossoms as it pleases God! Embrace gratitude. Make it a daily practice and see the Glory of God manifest!

REFLECTION:

Milagros, while experiencing abuse and devastation, found God's strength in her soul. She serves organizations and professionals in overcoming barriers and building sustainable advocacy efforts. Milagros aims to empower others through writing and speaking.

Social Media FB | IG: Lotus BeYouTy

THE GRACE OF GOD

Cheryl Swanson

"For it is by grace you have been saved; through Faith and this is not from yourself. It is the gift of God not by works, so that no one can boast."

Ephesians 2:8-9

I was raised in the church and received the Holy Spirit at the age of eight years old. I didn't understand what was happening to me at that time. Then, I grew into a teenager and my eyes were open to all kinds of things I figured were a better and easier way to live. This cost me a lot of pain and problems I really did not need in my life. Even to this day, I still have problems getting past a lot of it. Most of it came from me not listening to my mother and father. If I would have listened, I would have never entered the prison system. However, that is where I really got to get to know the Lord and allowed him take control of my heart and life. It also showed me I was not alone, and I had someone to fight for me. He carried me through the system. So, from then on, each time I prayed, these are the words that would come to me, even to this day, "Lord give me strengthen to overcome these obstacles in my way in the name of Jesus.

REFLECTION:

____

____

____

____

____

____

____

____

____

____

Cheryl Swanson is a native of Atlanta Ga. She is the mother 5 girls and grandmother of 23. When she is not helping the community through outreach you can find her singing and dancing. Here favorite chapter in the bible is Psalms 35.

Social Media FB | IG: Cheryl Swanson

HIS PLAN, NOT MINE

Queen Of Collaboration: Angela Thomas Smith

"**For I know the plans I have for you,**" declares the LORD, "plans to prosper you and not to harm you..." Jeremiah 29:11 (NIV) ,

Jeremiah.1:5, "**Before I formed thee in the belly, I knew thee**; and before thou camest forth out of the womb I sanctified thee, and I ordained thee a prophet unto the nations."

Dec 2012, I remember this scripture being dropped in my spirit while on a journey of uncertainty and the trying of my faith. May 7, 2014, I was shot at point blank range with a sawed-off shotgun. The doctors said, "It may be months before you can walk again." But God! I walked out of that hospital. Glory be to GOD! I stood on his word, even when I couldn't understand why such a thing had happened to me. May 2016, I lost six family members, three of them to suicide.

I was broken and ready to throw in the towel, but GOD opened my eyes and ears. He mended and molded me into the woman he had purposed me to be from the beginning. I had to endure, so I could be here today to reassure you his word is true. It is a lamp unto my feet and a light unto my pathway. He is my guide, and he orders my steps. No matter what it looks like in the natural, he gets all my praises. I am steadfast and unmovable. God is at work in you and me. He is calling us to delight ourselves in him so he can make us new. He is stirring up those gifts, trying to take us to a new level, but we must humble ourselves and allow him to work.

He is REPAIRING you now. Allow yourself to HEAL and the HURT to leave!

REFLECTION:

____

____

____

____

____

____

____

____

Angela Thomas Smith is a purpose pusher, radio personality, magazine owner, author of 24 books, Certified L.I.F.E. coach, and founder of AAALAC (African American authors literacy awareness campaign) Email: 3alac2016@gmail.com

Instagram: angelaqueenofcollaboration **Website:** aspiringauthorsmagazine.godaddysites.com

MAKE THE PROCLAMATION

Dr. Derashay Zorn, Kingdom Strategist

"the Lord moved the heart of Cyrus king of Persia to make a proclamation throughout his realm and also to put it in writing:"

Ezra 1:1 NIV

When you begin to proclaim in the earth what God has placed in your heart to fulfill, you will start attracting destiny helpers to get it done. I know we are often told not to tell what we are doing because people believe others will steal our dreams or vision. I'm not going to say that there may not be people who will try to copy your dream. Even if they did, I can guarantee you it will not make the same influence or impact as when you implemented it because you have the original blueprint.

In the book of Ezra, God told the king to make a proclamation throughout his kingdom and put it in writing. King Cyrus obeyed God and began to send out the proclamation within the land. His obedience brought forth the fruit of God's word because it attracted those who God had preordained to get the work done. Many are frustrated because they are being silent within their assignment, or they are selecting who they want to assist them in completing it. Release in the earth what God has placed in your heart so who He has chosen can get in place and manifest the word of the Lord.

Dear God, thank you for filling my heart with your words to proclaim in the earth so they will attract my destiny helpers, in the name of Jesus, amen.

REFLECTION:

Kingdom Strategist, Blueprint Builder, and Spiritual Midwife, Dr. Derashay Zorn is an international business coach and best-selling author. She helps the faith-based community magnetize and monetize their influence and impact by creating profitable brands that develop long-lasting relationships with products and services their ideal client loves.

Discover how she can take your message and develop your next book, membership program, course, educational platform, coaching program, and more by visiting https://px.fyi/teawiththestrategist.

Social Media FB | IG: kingdom.strategist **Website:** www.derashay.com

WORKPLACE PRAYER

Melissa Baines

"Commit everything you do to the Lord. Trust him, and he will help you. He will make your innocence radiate like the dawn,and the justice of your cause will shine like the noonday sun. Be still in the presence of the Lord, and wait patiently for him to act. Don't worry about evil people who prosper or fret about their wicked schemes. Stop being angry! Turn from your rage! Do not lose your temper— it only leads to harm. For the wicked will be destroyed, but those who trust in the Lord will possess the land.

Psalm 37:5-9 NLT

Lord, I will be patient and await the answer. I know You hear, and You are not blind. Thank you that the knowledge of the glory of the Lord will fill my workplace. Lord, I will be silent before You. I am in awe of You. Repeat Your wonderous works. Give me the plan that I may write it down plain and understand. You are said to be a mystery. However, You reveal Yourself and Your Ways to those who will listen, those who listen and eagerly await Your deliverance. Nevertheless, I will praise You in the wait. My spirit will spring up in anticipation of your wonderous works, even Your salvation. Amen! It is so!

REFLECTION:

Melissa, more familiarly known as Missy/Sis. Missy, considers herself as one The Lord is completing His Good Work in. Among her many Kingdom Assignments, her most meaningful and heartwarming are that of an adoptive and God mother, missionary, and exhorter. The Lord uses Missy strategically in diverse relationships and networking, where her faith is shared freely.

Social Media FB | Melissa (Missy) Baines

GOD'S MIRROR

Carla Wade

Therefore if any man be in Christ, he is a new creature: old things are passed away; behold, all things are become new.

2 Corinthians 5:17

When you look into the mirror, who do you see? Often, it's a reflection of life looking back at you. You see, life is like a roller coaster. You have your ups, and you have your downs.

You have your peaks, and you have your valleys. You are only in a temporary state of being.

Sometimes we look to others for validation, but only you can write the pages of your book. No one can tell your story better than you can.

You are not what you have been through.

Your today does not define your tomorrow, and where you begin does not indicate where you will finish. How can you testify if you don't have a testimony, and how can you tell people about God if you do not know him for yourself?

After you have been tried and gone through the fire, give God all the glory. You do not look like what you have been through. You have been beautifully and wonderfully made in the image of Christ, our lord and savior.

REFLECTION:

Carla Wade is a native of New Orleans, LA. She accepted Christ at an early age. Carla is a graduate of Cameron College, (ACE) Accredited Christian Education, and Aaron's Beard School of the Prophets. Ordained as an evangelist and a prophet, she has a heart for God's people. She is also the founder of King's Connection, International and Let's Talk Woman 2 Woman.

Social Media Twitter: @CarlaWOG

I CAN SHOW YOU INCREDIBLE THINGS

Dr. Ericka L. McKnight

"To whom much given, much is required"

Luke 12:48.

If you have heard that line of wisdom, you know it means we are held responsible for what we have. If we have been blessed with talents, wealth, knowledge, time, and the like, it is expected that we share it with others.

Our wants or needs for much comes from our desire to live our best life. In doing so, we must be mindful of others who have the same desire. For example, if my glass of water is filled to the brim with ice, I typically dump it out or ask if someone else needs some ice. No need to waste the ice if someone can use it. The same rule applies to having much and being required to share with others. "The blessing of the Lord, it makes us rich, and he adds no sorrow with it" (Proverbs 10:22).

As God fills your barns, cups, bank accounts, and lifestyle, be prepared to blessed others! I promise you will see your life transform instantly, and doors will open for you to share your story.

Dear God, decrease me so that you will increase in me. Enlarge my territory and bless me indeed. Because I seek you and love you, I thank you that no good thing will be held from me, in Jesus' name, amen.

REFLECTION:

____

____

____

____

____

____

Dr. Ericka L. McKnight is a mother of three, international best-selling, multi award-winning author of her latest book, Silence the Noise: Uninstalling Negativity trilogy. She is a also speaker, entrepreneur, and the owner of ELM School of Real Estate, the first female African American to own a Real Estate School in the southeastern region. In addition, she is the owner of the ELM Realty firm. Dr. Ericka has been featured in ELLE, Pride, Southern Christian Writers, and Humani magazines, just to name a few.

FB | IG: @elmschoolofrealestate **Web:** elmschoolofrealestate.com

DIVINE INTERRUPTION

Dr. Derashay Zorn, Kingdom Strategist

"So Haman took the robe and the horse, arrayed Mordecai and led him on horseback through the city square, and proclaimed before him, "Thus shall it be done to the man whom the king delights to honor!"

Esther 6:11 NKJV

There's a *divine interruption* God is doing in your life. He is interrupting the plan of the enemy against your marriage, children, family, ministry, business, health, finances, education, and more. Your labor has not been in vain. God has heard your cry just as He heard Mordecai in the book of Esther, and He is bringing your enemy to shame. God is turning it around for your good and in your favor.

God has interrupted the enemy's plan to destroy you. Don't get discouraged about what your adversary is doing and don't give up. God is preparing the right opportunity to honor you in the presence of your enemies.

Prayer: *Dear Lord, I thank you for disrupting the plans of the enemy in my life. Give me the strength to trust you in the heat of the battle so I may endure to the end, to see the victory you have before me, in Jesus' name, amen.*

REFLECTION:

Kingdom Strategist, Blueprint Builder, and Spiritual Midwife, Dr. Derashay Zorn is an international business coach and best-selling author. She helps the faith-based community magnetize and monetize their influence and impact by creating profitable brands that develop long-lasting relationships with products and services their ideal client loves.

Discover how she can take your message and develop your next book, membership program, course, educational platform, coaching program, and more by visiting https://px.fyi/teawiththestrategist.

Social Media FB | IG: kingdom.strategist **Website:** www.derashay.com

BE ENCOURAGED!

Dr. Sylathia Hollie

"Be strong and of good courage; be not afraid."

Joshua 1:9

Most of us could agree that the current crisis has given us plenty of reasons to lose heart and give up on our dreams. Upon returning home from what I considered to be the best vacation I have experienced in recent years, I received the devasting news that my youngest sister had passed away suddenly. I immediately went from elation to deep sorrow. Many of you can relate. You've experienced times of great celebration, then confronted by an unexpected adversity. The Lord gave me a word. He said to be of good courage! The word courage means to have confidence and hope. Regardless of the challenge or hardship, I encourage you to keep going and keep dreaming big! God's plans don't change when life does. He is with you, and you cannot fail.

REFLECTION:

Dr. Sylathia Hollie is a conference speaker, minister, talk show host and author! She specializes in motivating women to walk in their calling.

Social Media FB: @drlacey55 **IG:** @drsylathia

TRUST GOD'S WAY

Dr. Derashay Zorn, Kingdom Strategist

"Trust in the Lord with all your heart, And lean not on your own understanding;"

Proverbs 3:5

God has declared the plans for your business, and it's essential you trust Him in its direction. The path God created for us is often contrary to the way we won't to go. However, it's in the best interest of the company to follow God's directions, especially since He is all-knowing. As we allow God to lead, we must trust God's way and not lean on our understanding. The word tells us that God's way is not our way. His way is much higher than ours. Therefore, it's time to take off the brakes of resistance and follow the way of the Lord. He will not lead you astray but lead you to the destination, according to the Jeremiah 29:11 plan.

Entrepreneur Thought: What are your thoughts on leaning to your own understanding in business matters and transactions?

Entrepreneur Prayer: *Lord, give me the strength to trust your way in my business, in Jesus' name, amen.*

REFLECTION:

Kingdom Strategist, Blueprint Builder, and Spiritual Midwife, Dr. Derashay Zorn is an international business coach and best-selling author. She helps the faith-based community magnetize and monetize their influence and impact by creating profitable brands that develop long-lasting relationships with products and services their ideal client loves.

Discover how she can take your message and develop your next book, membership program, course, educational platform, coaching program, and more by visiting https://px.fyi/teawiththestrategist.

Social Media FB | IG: kingdom.strategist **Website:** www.derashay.com

INTERCESSORY PRAYER WARRIORS NEEDED

Doris G. Barren

"I urge you first of all to pray for all people, ask God to help them, intercede on their behalf, and give thanks for them"

I Timothy 2:1.

Prayer is a form of communication or talking to God. Prayer is a means of getting things from God. Amazing things can be accomplished in your life by praying regularly. Each day we should seek God and take our concerns to Him early in the morning while he can be found. We should pray for our families, finances, church, personal problems, and daily activities. I am an intercessory prayer warrior, one whom God has entrusted to stand in the gap for souls. All people are precious to God and need to be saved, and in his timing, he will bring it to pass. If no one prays for them or intercedes on their behalf, they will continue to be lost. Psalms 5:3 says, "Make your requests known unto God. Lay it before him and wait patiently for his answer." Sometimes we must also add fasting with prayer for certain situations, to tear down strongholds.

Keep asking and seeking and he will bring it to pass.

I'm a living witness!

REFLECTION:

Doris Barren has lived 70 blessed years and has been married for 50. She has three children, nine grandchildren, and three great grandchildren.

Doris is also a prayer warrior for the Kingdom of God!

Social Media FB: Doris Barren

LAUNCH INTO THE DEEP

Dr. Derashay Zorn, Kingdom Strategist

"When He had stopped speaking, He said to Simon, 'Launch out into the deep and let down your nets for a catch.'"
Luke 5:4 NKJV

Simon Peter and his business partners were out on the sea toiling all night to catch some fish. As professional fishermen, they knew when, where, and how to make their catch successfully. Unfortunately, this night they found themselves not producing favorable results as they engaged in their normal routine. Then, Jesus comes on the scene and tell Simon to "Launch out into the deep and let down your nets for the catch." Like the fishermen, many are very talented and knowledgeable in what they do. However, they are not producing the results they desire. This could be due to remaining in familiar and comfortable or unwanted places, which we will identify as the shallow waters. God is calling you to "Launch into the Deep" so that you can experience the fullness of His word. This means you must leave what's familiar and comfortable to bear greater results because there are people who are waiting for you to show up with your talents, understand your worth, and are willing to pay for it. Come out of the shallow places, away from shallow people, and launch out into the deep.

Entrepreneur Thought: Where are the places you have not explored, but they need the service or product you have to offer?

Entrepreneur Prayer: *Father, thank you for leading me into places and before people that yield results in their lives and minds, in Jesus' name, amen.*

REFLECTION:

____

____

____

____

____

Kingdom Strategist, Blueprint Builder, and Spiritual Midwife, Dr. Derashay Zorn is an international business coach and best-selling author. She helps the faith-based community magnetize and monetize their influence and impact by creating profitable brands that develop long-lasting relationships with products and services their ideal client loves.

Discover how she can take your message and develop your next book, membership program, course, educational platform, coaching program, and more by visiting https://px.fyi/teawiththestrategist.

Social Media FB | IG: kingdom.strategist **Website:** www.derashay.com

WALKING IN YOUR PROPHETIC DESTINY

Dr. Rolanda S. Watson

"For I know the plans that I have for you, declares the Lord; Plans to prosper you and not harm you. Plans to give you hope and a future"

Jeremiah 29:11.

There's a prophetic destiny God has for each one of you. There is a prophetic destiny God has for each of you, individually and collectively as a family, a church, a city, and as a nation. Everything you are doing in your life right now, may or may not be everything God will have you do in this lifetime. He will equip you with what you need to lead you into your purpose and His plan. If it is your destiny to work with children, God will anoint you and give you a love for children in your heart. If it's your destiny to evangelize, God will put a burden in your soul to see people saved and set free. In many instances, a person's gift will help define his or her calling in life. Many times, we settle for this job or that one to pay bills or make ends meet, never really finding the fulfillment God intended from the beginning. Just as God told the children of Israel in Jeremiah 29:11, He also told Jeremiah his purpose in chapter 1: 4-5. If He told Jeremiah his destiny, why wouldn't He tell you and me? Child of God you are in an excellent place in God; this is time to begin seeking a stronger and intimate relationship with Him through His Son, Jesus Christ. Not only will He reveal who Christ is, but who you are. Through prayer and supplication, Holy Spirit will help you discover and not decide your purpose, to prevent you from wasting time walking in the wilderness for 40 years, trying to become a nurse, when He equipped you to be a surgeon. Finally, the main reason He wants you to walk in your purpose is to get glory out of your life. God will get the GLORY; the people you reach along the way will get the BLESSING; and you'll have the continued JOY OF GOD'S SALVATION. Be Blessed in Jesus' name!

REFLECTION:

___

___

___

___

___

Dr. Watson is an international best-selling author, certified life coach, and entrepreneur. Residing in Atlanta, she is committed to empowering women in the areas of business and ministry.

Social Media: FB: Rolanda S. Watson **IG:** @Rolandaswatson

BECOME FORTIFIED

Dr. Derashay Zorn, Kingdom Strategist

> *"And I will make you to this people a fortified bronze wall; And they will fight against you, But they shall not prevail against you; For I am with you to save you And deliver you," says the Lord."*
>
> Jeremiah 15:20

To position your business for success, you must become fortified in the Lord. Your strength, support, and success is all in Him. When you fortify yourself in people, your business is doomed to fail.

Fortify is defined as a) to strengthen and secure, b) to give physical strength, courage, or endurance, c) to add mental or moral strength and d) to strengthen or enhance by the addition of some substance or ingredient.

When your business is fortified in the Lord, God will give you the victory over a matter, when things come to destroy it. Only in Him can your business grow and do everything He has called it to do. Let God be your source in all things as He is the only one who is 100% faithful.

Entrepreneur Thought: What things have you trusted in that led you to defeat? What are you doing now to change the outcome from defeat to victory?

Entrepreneur Prayer: *Dear God, only in you shall I depend for strength, security, and success. You are my fortress, in Jesus' name, amen*

REFLECTION:

Kingdom Strategist, Blueprint Builder, and Spiritual Midwife, Dr. Derashay Zorn is an international business coach and best-selling author. She helps the faith-based community magnetize and monetize their influence and impact by creating profitable brands that develop long-lasting relationships with products and services their ideal client loves.

Discover how she can take your message and develop your next book, membership program, course, educational platform, coaching program, and more by visiting https://px.fyi/teawiththestrategist.

Social Media FB | IG: kingdom.strategist **Website:** www.derashay.com

YOU ARE ANOINTED

Dr. Cecilia Jackson

"The sovereign LORD has filled me with his Spirit and has sent me to bring good news to the poor, to heal the broken-hearted, to announce release to captives and freedom to those bound and to proclaim the time has come when the LORD"

Isa 61:1-4

There is an anointing God has placed upon your life, equipping you to accomplish what HE has assigned you to do in his Kingdom on earth.

Nurture your assignment, your dream, and don't let anyone snuff it out, stamp it out, drown it out, talk you out of it, nor speak fear into your mind and heart about it. One of my dreams since age 12 was to become a writer and public speaker. Therefore, I wrote from age 12 until now. Manifestation of the dream came!

Dreams and assignments manifest when you cooperate with the vision within you placed there by the Lord. THINK, DREAM, PERSEVERE, BECOME!

As stated in Isaiah 61: 1-4, the Lord will use YOU during this era to build and establish the lives of others. Walk forward in confidence, even with imperfections. He has anointed you.

REFLECTION:

____

____

____

____

____

____

____

____

____

____

Dr. Cecilia Jackson is: 1) Official Delegate of the United Nations for the Cause of Women 2) Author of 36 professional publications 3) Founder and Co-Provost of the "I AM" College of Ministry 4) Founder of Seasoned Anointed Oil for Regional Women in Leadership 5) State Certified Educator 6) Radio Show 7) spiritual Mid-wife Email: drcjackson3712@gmail.com

Social Media FB | IG: I AM Productions Publishing

Website: iamfellowshipministries.net

"NO MORE DELAY," SAYS THE LORD!!!!

Dr. Derashay Zorn, Kingdom Strategist

"And swore by Him who lives forever and ever, who created heaven and the things that are in it, the earth and the things that are in it, and the sea and the things that are in it, that there should be delay no longer"

Rev. 10:6 NKJV

We declare, "No more delayed promises. No more delayed thoughts. No more delayed actions. No more delayed planning. No more delayed execution. No more delayed assignment. No more delayed resources. In Jesus' name."

Too many have been delayed in their assignment unto the Lord. There is a quickening of the spirit going forth in the land of the living that has broken the chain and bondage of delay. Do not move with haste on that in which God has fashion in your heart because there is a synchronized waved that has gone forth. If you do not move with the flow of the spirit of God, you are going to place yourself back in a holding pattern. For those who flow with the Spirit of the Lord, you going to find favor, open doors, and blessings in the land of the living because the alignment of all things is in order so that you can possess your inheritance, your breakthrough from the Lord.

Move, conquer and possess, for the Spirit of the Lord is with you!

Prayer: *Father we break the spirit of fear, hesitation, and procrastination, in the mighty name of Jesus. We declare every cord cut and destroyed, in the mighty name of Jesus, amen.*

REFLECTION:

____

____

____

____

Kingdom Strategist, Blueprint Builder, and Spiritual Midwife, Dr. Derashay Zorn is an international business coach and best-selling author. She helps the faith-based community magnetize and monetize their influence and impact by creating profitable brands that develop long-lasting relationships with products and services their ideal client loves.

Discover how she can take your message and develop your next book, membership program, course, educational platform, coaching program, and more by visiting https://px.fyi/teawiththestrategist.

Social Media FB | IG: kingdom.strategist **Website:** www.derashay.com

LONELY BUT NEVER ALONE

Janice D. Shaw

"Lo I am with you always, even to the end of the age"

Matthew 28:20.

Loneliness causes people to feel empty, alone, sometimes unwanted, and it even causes pain. But even in our loneliness, we are never alone, for lo He is with us always, even to the end of the age! That means regardless of any situation or circumstance, He is with us at all times!

Sometimes, He calls us to a place of being alone to draw us closer to Him. It's His desire to bring us to a deeper level of intimacy in Him. When we are lonely, we don't even realize we need alone time with God. Recently, God took me into a place of loneliness, to shut down my busyness, in order to heal my brokenness. He wanted His voice to be the loudest voice I heard, canceling out the voice of the enemy. Sometimes we use busyness as a crutch to hide pain and loneliness.

It was in that place that God reminded me who I am and whose I am! He said, "Baby girl, I've got you! Before you were formed in your mother's womb, I had purpose for you! I know the plans I have for you, and they are good! What feels like a wilderness experience is all a part of your process, shaping you and molding you into the woman I've already ordained you to be. Remember, it's okay to feel lonely, but in me, you are never alone!

REFLECTION:

Janice D. Shaw is the founder of She is Clothed International, Owner/CEO of She is Clothed by JaniceDenice online boutique, ordained minister, teacher, prophetic psalmist, and worship leader.

Social Media FB @SheisClothedIntl **Website:**Sheisclothedintl.org

IS LOVE INCORPORATED?

LaCrecia V. McCree

"And now these three remain: faith, hope, and love. But the greatest of these is love."

1 Cor. 13:13

It didn't take much convincing of the 5-year-old me, that someday I would adopt. My grandmother had five children, and some day, so would I. At the age of 5, I watched as my mother took in one of my teenage uncle's friends. I would often times go with my grandmother to her sister's house, and one day there were two children there for me to play with. I later learned they were adopted by my great aunt. And, like my aunt and my grandmother I couldn't wait for the day to adopt.

At age 28, I uprooted myself from Kentucky and planted myself in Georgia. I felt guilty that the children I was created to adopt were waiting on me, possibly being mistreated and lonely. I missed the children I never knew, like they were already a part of me. I joined the church that I'd been attending. At that time, I felt certain, at 32, I'd missed my chance to adopt. But God had other plans for it to manifest. My church hosted an event for families to learn more the foster/adoptions process in Georgia. Pure and genuine religion in the sight of God the father means caring for orphans and widows in their distress and refusing to let the world corrupt you, James 1:27.

I knew I was chasing my calling, that ONE THING the Lord planted in me at the ripe age of five. By age 36, my two daughters moved into my home. At that time, they were 11 and 14 years old. We have had many amazing moments, but we've also had many rocky ones as well. I learned early on that "hurt people, hurt people," and my girls were in pain. I also learned that as a parent you will come face to face with your child's pain, and you must be strong enough to endure it. We had to relocate when things became too difficult for one of my girls. My oldest daughter became a habitual runaway, and I became angry with God transitioning me into this new being. I then had two daughters, was laid off from my job, pregnant, on bed rest, and wondering why the process hadn't gone as smooth as I'd imagined.

REFLECTION:

LaCrecia V. McCree is a mother, sister, and friend. She is also an author and an advocate for the homeless and abandoned.

PIECES OF MY HEART

Melissa Baines

"He heals the brokenhearted and binds up their wounds"

Psalm 147:3.

Lord, please help me to find the pieces of my heart.

I believe I left some with the one who promised to love me forever…

I left some with the one who "called himself" Your son…

I'm sure I left some with the one who never even noticed me…

I left some, unfortunately, with the one from whom I had to run. And I couldn't help but leave some with those dear ones who left me, by no choice of their own – most, to go to be with You.

Like puzzle pieces in a frame, You present my heart back to me; piece by piece, as a glorious picture, beautifully framed by Your Presence.

Because, actually, they were never lost…

They were found safe and secure, captured, stowed away, and held within my very own place, Your Heart. Amen…

REFLECTION:

___

___

___

___

___

___

___

___

___

Melissa, more familiarly known as Missy/Sis. Missy, considers herself as one The Lord is completing His Good Work in. Among her many Kingdom Assignments, her most meaningful and heartwarming are that of an adoptive and God mother, missionary, and exhorter. The Lord uses Missy strategically in diverse relationships and networking, where her faith is shared freely.

Social Media FB | Melissa (Missy) Baines

SOW YOUR SEED

Dr. Derashay Zorn, Kingdom Strategist

"A sower went out to sow his seed. … But others fell on good ground, sprang up, and yielded a crop a hundredfold." When He had said these things He cried, "He who has ears to hear, let him hear!"

Luke 8:5-8 NKJV

Every entrepreneur should have a growth and development plan for their business. This plan should include some aspect of spreading the good news about what God has given you to solve your potential client's problems. You should be planting seeds about your brand in the hearts through some form of marketing effort. You can do this through your branded attire, speech, or materials so you can imprint your business in the minds of others. This effort in planting seeds about your business can change your business' bottom line with minimal effort. The next time you consider purchasing something to parade someone else's brand, consider having something customized to sow your seeds and attract your ideal client.

As you sow your seed about your business, there will be good ground it falls upon. Your ideal client will be attracted to your brand through your marketing efforts. Because you showed up and sowed, you shall reap the harvest. Remember, you cannot grow where you do not sow.

Entrepreneur Thought: Where are you sowing your seed for your business?

Entrepreneur Prayer: *Father, guide me to the places to sow seeds that will produce a harvest in the lives of others, in Jesus' name, amen.*

REFLECTION:

____

____

____

____

____

Kingdom Strategist, Blueprint Builder, and Spiritual Midwife, Dr. Derashay Zorn is an international business coach and best-selling author. She helps the faith-based community magnetize and monetize their influence and impact by creating profitable brands that develop long-lasting relationships with products and services their ideal client loves.

Discover how she can take your message and develop your next book, membership program, course, educational platform, coaching program, and more by visiting https://px.fyi/teawiththestrategist.

Social Media FB | IG: kingdom.strategist **Website:** www.derashay.com

GRATITUDE

Dr. Phyllis Pelzer

"And we know that all things work together for good to them that love God, to them who are called according to his purpose."

Romans 8:28

When we focus on the scripture of the day, we can certainly know that no matter what we may encounter in life, God is working it out for our good. I can recall starting over again, and my son and I were moving into a new apartment. I didn't have much furniture, but we had a television. Oprah Winfrey was on, and someone had just asked her what she contributed to her success. I stopped in my tracks to eagerly listen to her response, and she said, *"God gave me a little, and I thanked Him for that. Then, He gave me a little more, and I thanked Him for that."* Wow! The formula of God and Gratitude will positively influence your life!

Meditate and Pray ~ "Father God, Thank You for helping me to maintain an attitude of gratitude, knowing You are in control of my life. In Jesus' name, amen.

REFLECTION:

Dr. Phyllis Pelzer earned her Doctorate Degree of Theology. She is an ordained minister, empowerment mentor, author, podcaster and entrepreneur.

Social Media: FB Phyllis Pelzer | **IG** drphyl07

Website: www.ppconsultingenterprises.com

BE STILL AND KNOW, GOD IS WORKING IT OUT FOR YOU

Sharon Dawson-McElveen

"Fear not, for I am with you; Be not dismayed, for I am your God. I will strengthen you. Yes I will help you."

Isaiah 41:18

Looking back, I see how God has brought me through. Years ago, I was homeless with two children. Everything we owned was packed in black trash bags. I was in disbelief, but it was real. I felt maybe God was angry with me and had forgotten me.

Although I could not see it, God was working things out on my behalf. While homeless, I drew closer to God. Although we sought refuge at a shelter, God used me to begin a Bible Study. During this time, He was training and preparing me for my future. "Fear not, for I am with you."

Right now, you might be going through something, but I want to encourage you to be still and know that God is working it out for you. Out of my time of homelessness, little did I know that one day it would become my vocation and my work within the ministry.

I encourage you to not be dismayed by your circumstances, for the very thing that appears to be a hindrance or hardship will become your purpose to serve others. Who will you go back and help today?

REFLECTION:

Born and raised in New York City, Sharon felt a calling on her life as a young girl. Pastor Sharon holds a master's degree in Pastoral Care and Christian Counseling. She is the founder of Rose of Sharon Street Outreach Ministries, LLC. She serves as the Pastor over the outreach ministries at her church, where she leads her team in serving the community and those under bridges.

Social Media FB: Sharon Dawson McElveen

PRAYER FOR CONFORMITY

Melissa Baines

"God's servant must not be argumentative, but a gentle listener and teacher who keeps cool, working firmly but patiently with those who refuse to obey. You never know how or when God might sober them up with a change of heart and a turning to the truth, enabling them to escape the devil's trap, where they are caught and held captive, forced to run his errands."

2 Timothy 2:24-25

I pray I might not be argumentative, a gentle listener and God-inspired teacher who keeps their cool, working firmly, but patiently with those who refuse to obey what they know in their hearts to be what is true and right. I thank You, Lord, in advance for the day You sober up, convict and change the hearts of all my loved ones - friends and family. I pray you equip them to quickly escape the devil's traps, where they have been caught, chained, weighed down, deceived, and convinced to do his bidding - not really doing things and making decisions on their own as the enemy would have them to think. In Jesus' name and by His matchless blood, amen!

REFLECTION:

Melissa, more familiarly known as Missy/Sis. Missy, considers herself as one The Lord is completing His Good Work in. Among her many Kingdom Assignments, her most meaningful and heartwarming are that of an adoptive and God mother, missionary, and exhorter. The Lord uses Missy strategically in diverse relationships and networking, where her faith is shared freely.

Social Media FB | Melissa (Missy) Baines

LET YOUR BRILLIANCE SHINE

Dr. Derashay Zorn, Kingdom Strategist

"You are the light of the world. A city that is set on a hill cannot be hidden. Nor do they light a lamp and put it under a basket, but on a lampstand, and it gives light to all who are in the house. Let your light so shine before men, that they may see your good works and glorify your Father in heaven. "

Mathew 5:14-16

There is too much greatness inside of you to allow your situation, circumstances, and people to dim your shine. Before you were in the womb of your mother, God preordained for you to do a good work for Him. It is God's desire to utilize you in your purpose to deliver His promise to others in the earth. Therefore, there are people waiting on you to show up, just like the Israelites were waiting for God to deliver His promise. God sent Moses to do the job. They didn't know it was going to be Moses, but he was God's choice before the foundation of the earth. People in the land are waiting for His promises to be delivered to them. They are waiting for you. They don't know you are the one who holds the key to unleashing them in their destiny. However, God knows, and He has given you everything you need to complete the task. It's time to move in purpose. When other see your good works, they will begin to glorify the Father.

Dear God, thank you for calling me out of hiding so I may shine for your glorification, in Jesus' name, amen.

REFLECTION:

____

____

____

____

____

____

____

Kingdom Strategist, Blueprint Builder, and Spiritual Midwife, Dr. Derashay Zorn is an international business coach and best-selling author. She helps the faith-based community magnetize and monetize their influence and impact by creating profitable brands that develop long-lasting relationships with products and services their ideal client loves.

Discover how she can take your message and develop your next book, membership program, course, educational platform, coaching program, and more by visiting https://px.fyi/teawiththestrategist.

Social Media FB | IG: kingdom.strategist **Website:** www.derashay.com

FATHER KNOWS BEST

Rhonda Hudson

For I know the thoughts that I think toward you, saith the Lord, thoughts of peace, and not of evil, to give you an expected end.

Jeremiah 29:11

My son was excited about being able to drive and own one of our cars as his own. My husband had to make a decision on which car he would give to him. Both cars were the same make and model. However, one vehicle was a newer, shiny, and had more options. The other vehicle was older, dull in color, and only had AM/FM radio. My son wanted the newer car. My husband, being a former mechanic, chose the older car because the newer one had a defect that would cost a lot of money to fix. Now that my son has been driving the older car for a few years without any major issues, he's glad his father knew what was best.

Just as an earthly father makes the best decisions for his children, our heavenly Father will do what's best for us also. God wants to give us the desires of our heart, so trust God and his word and know that you will receive His best.

REFLECTION:

Rhonda is a leader, teacher, and administrator. She enjoys serving and encouraging others and loves to see others achieve God's best for their lives.

Social Media FB | IG: Rhonda Autry Hudson

YOU HAVE BEEN REDEEMED

Sharon Dawson-McElveen

"But now, this is what the LORD says— he who created you, Jacob, he who formed you, Israel: 'Do not fear, for I have redeemed you; I have summoned you by name; you are mine."

Isaiah 43:1

We don't always say or do the right things, rather it is a thought or an action. For example, how about your thoughts when getting overlooked for a promotion or a position you qualified for. I can only imagine what you are thinking. Or perhaps, you may have said something to someone and realized you shouldn't have said that.

I once sent out a text and accidently sent it to the wrong person. I was venting and sent the message to the individual I was venting about. I knew for sure this was going to be the end of our relationship. How does God feel when we are disobedient by skipping prayer time or church service? Does this change God's mind about us? Absolutely not!

Just like my text message, the receiver understood my frustration and forgave me as I forgave myself. We were able to talk it through, and today our relationship is better than ever.

God has called you by your name. You have been summoned; trust that he can restore any relationships or situation you are facing today. He knows who you are.

REFLECTION:

____

____

____

____

____

____

____

Born and raised in New York City, Sharon felt a calling on her life as a young girl. Pastor Sharon holds a master's degree in Pastoral Care and Christian Counseling. She is the founder of Rose of Sharon Street Outreach Ministries, LLC. She serves as the Pastor over the outreach ministries at her church, where she leads her team in serving the community and those under bridges.

Social Media FB: Sharon Dawson McElveen

GET PAID FOR YOUR WISDOM

Dr. Derashay Zorn, Kingdom Strategist

"So King Solomon surpassed all the kings of the earth in riches and wisdom."

2 Chr. 9:22 NKJV

King Solomon was known as the most wise and wealthiest king in the world. One of his streams of income came from him consulting other kings. The other kings in the land understood that Solomon possessed something they needed for the advancement of their kingdom. The beauty was they were willing to pay for his knowledge, even though they were colleagues. They didn't feel it to be robbery to invest in obtaining his wisdom.

God has given you wisdom that other people need to possess so they can advance in their lives, ministries, or business. More than likely, you are already consulting, but you are doing it for free. This is because you and those you are consulting have not understood your value like King Solomons colleagues. It's time to know your worth and put a price take on it, so as you are helping others, your household can reap some benefits.

Dear God, thank you for the wisdom and skills you have given me to develop financial increase while helping others with solutions, in Jesus' name, amen.

REFLECTION:

Kingdom Strategist, Blueprint Builder, and Spiritual Midwife, Dr. Derashay Zorn is an international business coach and best-selling author. She helps the faith-based community magnetize and monetize their influence and impact by creating profitable brands that develop long-lasting relationships with products and services their ideal client loves.

Discover how she can take your message and develop your next book, membership program, course, educational platform, coaching program, and more by visiting https://px.fyi/teawiththestrategist.

Social Media FB | IG: kingdom.strategist **Website:** www.derashay.com

THE SCARLET THREAD

Dr. Rolanda S. Watson

"Let the redeemed of the Lord say so, whom he hath redeemed from the hand of the enemy"

Psalm 107: 2.

The topic of the blood is a scarlet thread that runs throughout the Bible, from Genesis to Revelation. From the beginning of the biblical record, God's dealing with humanity has been through the blood. If you are to access your Heavenly Father's presence, you must place the same importance on the blood as He does. With the understanding that life is in the blood and the penalty of sin is death, God established the principle that forgiveness comes only through the shedding of blood. In the Old Testament, the blood of animals was offered as a sacrifice for sin. Hebrews 8 details this process and describes it as the Old Covenant. In the New Testament, God sent Jesus, His only begotten, to shed His Blood for sin once and for all. The blood of Christ is described as the New Covenant. This makes the Old Covenant obsolete; it is no longer necessary for the blood of animals to be sacrificed for sin. By the Blood of Jesus, you have been set free. You have been redeemed and bought with a costly price. Once you've been redeemed by the Blood of the Lamb from the hand of the enemy, not only should you say so, but you are required to open your mouth and testify of His greatness. God expects you to become His witness in the earth. Therefore, in the same way, let your light shine before others, so they may see your good works and give glory to your Father who is in heaven (Matthew 5:16). Be Blessed in Jesus' name!

REFLECTION:

____

____

____

____

____

____

____

____

Dr. Watson is an international best-selling author, certified life coach, and entrepreneur. Residing in Atlanta, she is committed to empowering women in the areas of business and ministry.

Social Media: FB: Rolanda S. Watson **IG:** @Rolandaswatson

CONSIDER YOUR WAYS!!!!

Dr. Derashay Zorn, Kingdom Strategist

"Thus says the Lord of hosts: "Consider your ways!"

Haggai 1:7 (NKJV)

Many people want to blame the devil, the witches, warlocks, and more for their conditions, and neither of them have absolutely nothing to do with it. Your spiritual warfare breeds from within because of your own selfishness. You are after your own personal gain under the false pretense that you are doing it for the Lord. God sees your heart and knows your motives.

Repent unto the Lord and change your ways. Ask God to create in you a clean heart and renew in you a right spirit. It's time to be about your father's business. Stop taking care of yourself and leaving His work undone. God's people are sitting in ruin because of your selfish motives for personal gain. You will never progress, success will never overtake you, and you will never prosper until you be about your father's business. Repent before you are brought to ruins.

Turn the mirror on yourself and consider your way. Your conditions, circumstances, trials, and tribulations could be the work of your own ways. Have you considered what you have contributed to what's happening in your life right now?

Prayer: *Dear Lord, expose every way within me that doesn't line up with your word and teach me with your truth so that I may bear the fruit of your words, in Jesus' name, amen.*

REFLECTION:

____

____

____

____

____

____

Kingdom Strategist, Blueprint Builder, and Spiritual Midwife, Dr. Derashay Zorn is an international business coach and best-selling author. She helps the faith-based community magnetize and monetize their influence and impact by creating profitable brands that develop long-lasting relationships with products and services their ideal client loves.

Discover how she can take your message and develop your next book, membership program, course, educational platform, coaching program, and more by visiting https://px.fyi/teawiththestrategist.

Social Media FB | IG: kingdom.strategist **Website:** www.derashay.com

YOU CAN

Temecka Smith

"I can do all things through Christ, which strengthened me."

Philippians 4:13-

You can do all things. This is quoted but oftentimes not applied to our lives. I come to encourage you that with GOD "you can" do all things, according to his will for your life. "You are fearfully and wonderfully made," Psalms 139.14. You are equipped for what God has called you to do in the earth. Romans 8:30 tells us, "Moreover, whom he did predestinate, he also called: and whom he called, he also justified, and whom he justified, he also glorified." Smile and look in the mirror and say I can. When we come to know God, we begin to know his word, which is who he is. In the beginning was the Word, and the Word was with God, and the Word was God. In knowing God comes a trust. If he said it, you can do it. When we know God is capable of all things, we will take the limits off him and soar as eagles. Who would we all be in life if we trusted God and said, "I CAN."

REFLECTION:

____

____

____

____

____

____

____

____

____

____

Temecka Smith is an International Best Selling Author, Relationship Coach, Founder of Real Life Real Issues, Associate Pastor of Good Samaritan Center of Hope, and most of all, a servant of the most high God Jesus Christ. She works with individuals personally and corporately through her coaching program to equip and develop them in areas they lack, getting to the root of the issues through counseling courses, and much more. She has a passion for equipping wives and women in waiting with the tools to be all God called them as Mothers, Wives, Business owners, etc.

You can locate me at @temeckasmith/Facebook and Instagram

Social Media FB | IG: @temeckasmith

FULFILL YOUR VOWS TO THE LORD

Dr. Derashay Zorn, Kingdom Strategist

"If a man makes a vow to the Lord, or swears an oath to bind himself by some agreement, he shall not break his word; he shall do according to all that proceeds out of his mouth."

Num 30:2

God expects that we fulfill every word that comes out of our mouth. Our vows unto the Lord should be taken seriously, and we should follow through with them. Otherwise, we have caused our self to sin against God. As we are made in the same image and likeness of God, your word should not come back void unto him. Many have made vows unto the Lord and relented. It's time to go back and make due on our vow so we will no longer be sinning against Him.

Prayer: *Dear Lord, I repent for every vow I have broken unto you. Give me the strength to follow through with my words and the wisdom to not make a vow I don't intend to fulfill, in Jesus' name, amen*

REFLECTION:

____

____

____

____

____

____

____

____

____

____

Kingdom Strategist, Blueprint Builder, and Spiritual Midwife, Dr. Derashay Zorn is an international business coach and best-selling author. She helps the faith-based community magnetize and monetize their influence and impact by creating profitable brands that develop long-lasting relationships with products and services their ideal client loves.

Discover how she can take your message and develop your next book, membership program, course, educational platform, coaching program, and more by visiting https://px.fyi/teawiththestrategist.

Social Media FB | IG: kingdom.strategist **Website:** www.derashay.com

BRIGHTER DAYS ARE COMING

Carla Wade

"The suffering won't last forever."

1st Peter 5:10 MSG

Have you ever been driving, and it began to pour down raining? Your initial instinct is to pull over and wait for the rain to subside. You decide to drive on through it, and you discover that the sun is shining on the other side. See, that's how life is. Every day is not a day of roses and bliss. Trials and tribulations shall come. Situations will arise that may throw you a curveball. What's in your storehouse? Have you saved up for a rainy day? We must fast, pray, and stay in the word of God. The just shall live by faith, so we can't be moved by what we see. Even Jesus Christ, our Lord and Savior, was not exempt from troubles. We are not greater than Christ. We must be steadfast, immovable, always abounding in the work of the Lord. Look where God has brought you from. You can't stop here. There is no turning around. God knows your ending date. Your heavenly father will never leave you nor forsake you. Your brighter days are ahead of you.

REFLECTION:

____

____

____

____

____

____

____

____

____

____

Carla Wade is a native of New Orleans, LA. She accepted Christ at an early age. Carla is a graduate of Cameron College, (ACE) Accredited Christian Education, and Aaron's Beard School of the Prophets. Ordained as an evangelist and a prophet, she has a heart for God's people. She is also the founder of King's Connection, International and Let's Talk Woman 2 Woman.

Social Media FB | IG: ________________ **Website:** __________

PRAYER ON IDENTITY

Lillian Tinsley

"But ye are a chosen generation, a royal priesthood, an holy nation, a peculiar people; that ye should shew forth the praises of him who hath called you out of darkness into his marvellous light;"

1 Peter 2:9

Dear Heavenly Father, I praise you for there is no one like You. You are a mighty God, a wonderful savior, Prince of peace, a restorer, healer, and deliverer. Thank you, Lord, for loving us back to wholeness and for giving us the ability to see who we are in You. Thank you for awakening us to the realization of our identity and true worth. Lord, we have a heart of gratitude for you bringing us to this awareness, and we give you all glory and praise. It is in the mighty name of Jesus I pray, Amen.

REFLECTION:

Minister Lillian Jackson Tinsley is a native of Lakeland, Florida. She is a Counselor, Teacher, Mentor, Motivational Speaker, Psalmist, and Liturgical Dancer. Lillian is dedicated to serving the people of God. One of her greatest passions is to use her God-given abilities to snatch people out of the fire of hopelessness, insecurities, depression, and despair. She birthed Healing Heart's Personal Touch Ministries out of the pain and devastation of surviving rape and domestic violence. Lillian is the mother of two beautiful daughters, two grandchildren, and mother to many young adults that pursue excellence and wholeness in mind, body, and spirit. Ms. Tinsley has a MA degree in Mental Health and Marriage & Family Counseling from Webster University.

Social Media FB: | @ lillian.tinsley **IG:** lil_lillian01

RESTORATION BELONGS TO YOU

Dr. Derashay Zorn, Kingdom Strategist

"The Lord is my shepherd, I shall not be in want. He makes me lie down in green pastures, he leads me beside quiet waters, he restores my soul"

Psalm 23:1-3

On our life's journey, often the effect or impact of its events are overlooked or go unnoticed because of being preoccupied. While preoccupied with everything and everybody else, we often miss tending to ourselves (especially leaders). Those things that are overlooked or gone unnoticed are things that bring hindrances in our lives, ministries, business, relationships, and more. God wants to deal with the things that have kept us from moving forward into destiny. He had to bring King David to a place of solitude for his soul to be restored. Solitude is needed for restoration. Luke 5:16 says, "Jesus often withdrew to lonely places and prayed." If Jesus had to go into places of solitude often then surely, we must find ourselves there as well. Solitude with God is beneficial for where God is leading you. There are places you will never get to nor heights you will never reach if you don't learn the value of solitude.

In life, we all have acquired some wounds. To be effective in all that God places before us, it's important that we bring ourselves to a place of solitude for Him to heal us.

Prayer: *Dear Lord, give me the strength to trust you with everyone and everything else while you tend to my wounds, in Jesus' name, amen.*

REFLECTION:

____

____

____

____

____

____

Kingdom Strategist, Blueprint Builder, and Spiritual Midwife, Dr. Derashay Zorn is an international business coach and best-selling author. She helps the faith-based community magnetize and monetize their influence and impact by creating profitable brands that develop long-lasting relationships with products and services their ideal client loves.

Discover how she can take your message and develop your next book, membership program, course, educational platform, coaching program, and more by visiting https://px.fyi/teawiththestrategist.

Social Media FB | IG: kingdom.strategist **Website:** www.derashay.com

POWER TO BLESS OR WOUND

Lorna Wilson

"Death and Life are in the power of the tongue"

Proverbs 18:21.

Rise, ole tongue, rise.

Be careful where you lie.

What words will you speak? What secrets will you keep?

What truths will you tell? What power will you expel?

You are a strong muscle with extreme power. You can build speeches, books, roads, and towers.

Strike like lightening, cut like a knife. Be gentle as a lamb or quiet as the night. I prefer you give words life, words of happiness, strength and joy. Never of destruction or to destroy.

Putting them together like bricks, we use concrete because it sticks. Forming foundations that cannot be moved may cause bruising if misused. Speak highly of everyone or say nothing at all. You decide if your tongue rises or falls.

REFLECTION:

___

___

___

___

___

___

___

___

___

___

Lorna L. Wilson has a very unique and creative ability to take Biblical Scriptures and transform them into relatable, heartfelt, and passionate poetry, devotionals, and spoken words, as you will see in Influence 365.

Lorna's contribution and work appeal to all genres. It is fulfilling, creative and thought-provoking, always leaving the reader wanting to turn the next page to read more.

Social Media FB: Lorna Wilson

PRAY & LISTEN

Melissa Baines

> *"He that turneth away his ear from hearing the law, even his prayer shall be abomination."*
>
> Proverbs 28:9

God listened to Israel's ("our") prayer and gave them ("us") the Canaanites (anything that oppresses, attempts to overcome, sadden, anger, or burden us). They ("we can") destroy both them and their towns (annihilate those things at the root). This is a holy destruction (that's exactly what we are). They named the place Horma, Holy Destruction (Numbers 21:3).

As each night watch begins, GET UP and cry out in prayer. pour your heart out face-to-face with the master. Lift your hands high. Beg for the lives of your children and loved ones. Pray for those who are starving to death out on the streets, especially those outside The Kingdom) Lamentations 2:19.

However, God has no use for the prayers of the people who won't listen to Him, those who practice, meditate on, and become easily ensnared with disobedience (Proverbs 28:9).

REFLECTION:

____

____

____

____

____

____

____

____

____

Melissa, more familiarly known as Missy/Sis. Missy, considers herself as one The Lord is completing His Good Work in. Among her many Kingdom Assignments, her most meaningful and heartwarming are that of an adoptive and God mother, missionary, and exhorter. The Lord uses Missy strategically in diverse relationships and networking, where her faith is shared freely.

Social Media FB | Melissa (Missy) Baines

THE PRUDENT WIFE

Temecka Smith

"Houses and wealth are inherited from parents, but a prudent wife is from the Lord."

Proverbs 19:14 NIV

When I read this in scripture, I thought, *What is prudent?* I looked it up and understood she uses good judgement and common sense in handling practical matters. She has good character and is careful with her speech. Through experience, I've learned how to make a house a home. We must keep the sanctuary clean, not just naturally clean, but spiritually clean. I call it a sanctuary because marriage is a ministry. Your home should be the place he can't wait to get to because love is there, and peace is there. After a hard day's work, let him know how much you appreciate him and console him. What men want the most is to feel needed and appreciated. I share this to allow the little girl in you to be healed and whole, so you can be healthy for him. A prudent wife is a great blessing to both herself and her husband. A prudent wife also understands her husband may struggle with fears, even though he may look fearless. She knows he needs her support. A prudent wife is a gift from God who deserves much love and respect in return. Prudent wife, you're priceless.

REFLECTION:

____

____

____

____

____

____

____

____

Temecka Smith is an International Best Selling Author, Relationship Coach, Founder of Real Life Real Issues, Associate Pastor of Good Samaritan Center of Hope, and most of all, a servant of the most high God Jesus Christ. She works with individuals personally and corporately through her coaching program to equip and develop them in areas they lack, getting to the root of the issues through counseling courses, and much more. She has a passion for equipping wives and women in waiting with the tools to be all God called them as Mothers, Wives, Business owners, etc.

Social Media FB | IG: @temeckasmith

DO BUSINESS UNTIL HE COMES

Dr. Derashay Zorn, Kingdom Strategist

"So he called ten of his servants, delivered to them ten minas, and said to them, 'Do business till I come.'"

Luke 19:13 NKJV

Not in a million years did I ever dream about being a business owner. I was going to have an amazing career, purchase a house, get married, have children, and have enough money to sustain my lifestyle and leave for my children. After graduating with my undergrad and landing my first job in my field, I ended up birthing my first business in 2004 as I discovered my talents from God were a solution for others. This opened my eyes to understand that my gift will make room for me and generate multiple income streams. Since then, I have been doing business and allowing my gifts to multiply and create income streams. At that time, I had no idea God had provided me with a talent that could generate income. Therefore, before then, I was an unprofitable servant. Did you know God has given you a talent that solves a problem in the world, and you can get paid from it? He has provided you with everything you need to start and do business until He comes. When Jesus comes back, how will the usage of your talents be measured?

Entrepreneur Thoughts: What can you create or give instruction on that is a solution to a need?

Entrepreneur Prayer: *Father, I thank you for creative ideas and faith to diversify my talents to generate various income streams, in Jesus' name, amen.*

REFLECTION:

____

____

____

____

____

____

Kingdom Strategist, Blueprint Builder, and Spiritual Midwife, Dr. Derashay Zorn is an international business coach and best-selling author. She helps the faith-based community magnetize and monetize their influence and impact by creating profitable brands that develop long-lasting relationships with products and services their ideal client loves.

Discover how she can take your message and develop your next book, membership program, course, educational platform, coaching program, and more by visiting https://px.fyi/teawiththestrategist.

Social Media FB | IG: kingdom.strategist **Website:** www.derashay.com

BE INTENTIONAL

Dr. Dawn L. Cooper

"having an alabaster box…poured it on his head"

Matt. 26:7

Today, let's start our prayer, devotion, and walk while being an intentional blessing. If you are anything like me, most days I allow things to unfold as they will. I am often in prayer but rarely make an intentional effort to be a blessing to others.

The disciples found themselves in this position as well. They woke up one day and had no idea that was the day Jesus would be captured and later crucified. If they were intentional about being a blessing that day, perhaps they would have made a better effort to stay awake while Jesus prayed. However, it was with intention that Mary prepared the alabaster box and walked through the crowd, being scorned, to purposely and intentionally anoint the head of Jesus.

It is the days that I have prayed and sought opportunities to be a blessing that caused great fulfillment. It doesn't have to be anything grand. Go out of your way to hold a door, pay for someone's coffee behind you, send a note to cheer someone, or just smile.

I challenge you today to be an intentional blessing to those around you!

REFLECTION:

___

___

___

___

___

___

___

___

___

___

Dr. Dawn L. Cooper is an international best-selling author who resides in Indianapolis, Indiana. She is called by God to deliver biblical principles that build the Kingdom of God on Earth. Dr. Cooper is the mother of six and the grandmother of 12.

Social Media FB | IG: ______________ **Website:** __________

THE SKY IS THE LIMIT

Dr. Rolanda S. Watson

"I can do all things through Christ who strengthens me"

Philippians 4: 13.

As you believe God, believe also in yourself! You really can do all things through Christ who strengthens you (Phil.4:13). If you're not sure just yet, I propose that you spend time in prayer to get a sense of what you feel God has placed you in the earth to do. Search your heart to discern your passions. One thing that will help you to identify your main passion is to ask yourself, "What would I do even if I were not paid to do it?" Think about what gives you the greatest sense of fulfillment. What are you doing when you feel most alive? Then, to find the easiest way to get started, ask yourself, "How do I want to be remembered?" You can only become truly accomplished at something you love. Do not make money your goal. Instead, pursue the things you love and do them well, faithfully, and diligently! God rewards faithfulness and diligence. Once you have a general vision of what you want to do. It is important to define your goals. A goal is a dream with a deadline. Secondly, determine how much training or education you will need to accomplish your goals. Make sure you have SMART goals. SMART goals are: Specific~ Measurable~ Attainable~ Realistic~ Time-sensitive.

Once you have established your goals, pursue them with all your heart. The excellence you have in your life will be no greater than what you require of yourself! Make rules and set standards for yourself, maintain a positive attitude, and watch God bless you real good, in Jesus' name.

REFLECTION:

____

____

____

____

____

____

Dr. Watson is an international best-selling author, certified life coach, and entrepreneur. Residing in Atlanta, she is committed to empowering women in the areas of business and ministry.

Social Media: FB: Rolanda S. Watson **IG:** @Rolandaswatson

WIN FAVOR AND A GOOD NAME

Dr. Derashay Zorn, Kingdom Strategist

"Let not mercy and truth forsake you; Bind them around your neck, write them on the tablet of your heart, And so find favor and high esteem In the sight of God and man"

Proverbs 3:3-4 NKJV

If you find favor with the Lord, He will establish it within the land of the living for you. The things people do to obtain favor with man cost them more than it would ever cost them if they would work on establishing favor with God. The word declares you will win favor and a good name with God and man. God is listed first because it is He who establishes your favor with man. When you have obtained favor with God, He places you on the hearts and minds of individuals to be favorable unto you. When you have found favor with the Lord, the natural boundaries are rearranged just for you. Deuteronomy 6:10-11 is activated in your life. Abraham found favor with God in Genesis, and His descendants reaped the harvest. Man's favor is momentary, God's favor is eternal.

God requires a few things to win -- favor, a good name, and operating in love and faithfulness. These are requirements because love prompts obedience and faithfulness prompts commitment. When you are committed to God and what He has called you to do, He will supply the need and use others to support you. Without faith, it's impossible to please God. If we lack love, we will never have the faith to commit to the assignment.

Dear Lord, thank you for the lifestyle of love and faithfulness, in Jesus' name, amen.

REFLECTION:

____

____

____

____

____

____

Kingdom Strategist, Blueprint Builder, and Spiritual Midwife, Dr. Derashay Zorn is an international business coach and best-selling author. She helps the faith-based community magnetize and monetize their influence and impact by creating profitable brands that develop long-lasting relationships with products and services their ideal client loves.

Discover how she can take your message and develop your next book, membership program, course, educational platform, coaching program, and more by visiting https://px.fyi/teawiththestrategist.

Social Media FB | IG: kingdom.strategist **Website:** www.derashay.com

STANDING ON TRUTH

Dr. Dawn L. Cooper

"worship the father in spirit and in truth"

John 4:23

As you go about your day today, think of all that God is, His loving kindness, power, wisdom, and more. Then, realize this same God is living inside of you. Isn't that amazing? I think we know it but sometimes forget. Most times we forget while going through trials.

David had to remind himself of this when he was being hunted by Saul. I'm sure Joseph had to remind himself of this when he was falsely imprisoned. Even Jesus (the human side) had to remind Himself of this as he prayed, "Take this cup from me." When I read these accounts, I am reminded of just how good God is, and His truth shall save, protect, and cover us.

The Bible never speaks of facts but always truth. Fact is 1+1=2, but truth went beyond fact and allowed two fish to feed five thousand. Fact is, there were times I did not have enough gas in my car to reach my destination or enough money in my bank account to cover my bills. However, because I stood on the truth of God, I always reached my destination and bills were always paid.

Truth has no boundaries. Let's walk together in His truth today.

REFLECTION:

____

____

____

____

____

____

____

____

____

____

Dr. Dawn L. Cooper is an international best-selling author who resides in Indianapolis, Indiana. She is called by God to deliver biblical principles that build the Kingdom of God on Earth. Dr. Cooper is the mother of six and the grandmother of 12.

Social Media FB: @dlcooperauthor **Website:** https://dlcooperauthor.com

IT'S ME ~ PRAYER

Jeauniné S. Boyce

"Teach me, and I will hold my tongue: and cause me to understand wherein I have erred"

Job 6:24

Father, in the name of Jesus, I come to you humbled, with thanksgiving on my lips. You deserve all glory and honor. Not just because of who you are but also because of the many things you've blessed me with. First, I ask that you forgive me for the things I've done, knowing and unknowing. I ask that you continue to teach me the importance of forgiving! Father, anything that's not like you, I freely give! It's my desire to be like you, to love like you, to embrace like you, to forgive like you and to not judge because of you. I'm learning to acknowledge how I've contributed to the good and the bad in my life because, sometimes, it's me. I take full responsibility. I don't want to stand in your way or mine! Continue to teach me Lord because, sometimes, it's me! Continue to guide me so the way will be Your way and not mine because, sometimes, it's me. Father, I give You me. Amen.

REFLECTION:

____

____

____

____

____

____

____

____

____

____

Jeauniné S. Boyce is the founder of Heart Conversations with Jeauniné, LLC. She is a certified life coach, daughter, sister, mother, and grandmother.

Instagram: Conversations_with_Jeaunine

YOU GOT IT

Dr. Derashay Zorn, Kingdom Strategist

" He has filled them with skill to do all manner of work "

Exodus 35:35 NKJV

Did you know you have the skills others are looking for to enhance themselves, their businesses, or their ministries?

God has given you the skills to carry out specific tasks others are looking for to enhance them spiritually, personally, or professionally. You have those skills so you may help someone in their life journey and in turn make provision for your own.

It's time to stop doubting your abilities and use them to help others as God intended. No longer talk yourself out of showing off what God has place in you. People are waiting on you to show up and do what you are talented to do. Understand, you are among those God has filled with skills to get the job done. Others' assignments cannot be completed without you.

Entrepreneur Thought: How are you presenting your skills so those who are looking for what you have can find you?

Entrepreneur Prayer: *Father, I thank you for the skills to help others on their journey, in Jesus' name, amen.*

.REFLECTION:

____

____

____

____

____

____

____

____

Kingdom Strategist, Blueprint Builder, and Spiritual Midwife, Dr. Derashay Zorn is an international business coach and best-selling author. She helps the faith-based community magnetize and monetize their influence and impact by creating profitable brands that develop long-lasting relationships with products and services their ideal client loves.

Discover how she can take your message and develop your next book, membership program, course, educational platform, coaching program, and more by visiting https://px.fyi/teawiththestrategist.

Social Media FB | IG: kingdom.strategist **Website:** www.derashay.com

THE COURAGE TO SAY YES

Patricia Mahone

"For all the promises of God in him are yea, and in him Amen, unto the glory of God by us"

2 Corinthians 1:20 KJV.

What are you afraid of? What is that THING you've been thinking about doing but have talked yourself out of? Take a moment and look back. Think about the dreams and visions you had for your life. Did God lay something on your heart to do? Is there a business, a book, a ministry, or anything else that has been lying dormant inside you?

Well, today is your day to say YES. Say YES to the life God has prepared for you. Say YES to the freedom that resides in your purpose. Say YES to the path that God has already prepared for you. Say YES to the greatness that's ready to flow from you. That vision and dream God gave you may have you petrified but say YES and do it afraid. God is waiting for your YES.

REFLECTION:

Patricia Mahone is founder of Hidden Gems Consulting in Atlanta, GA. She's a wife, mother, mentor, and certified life coach.

Social Media FB | IG: @hidden_gem_unveiled **Website:** www.hgconsultsnow.com

FAITH IT TO MAKE IT

Alicia L. Amis

"Now faith is the assurance (title deed, confirmation) of things hoped for (divinely guaranteed), and the evidence of things not seen [the conviction of their reality—faith comprehends as fact what cannot be experienced by the physical senses]."

Hebrews 11:1 AMP

Faith is Definitely the second world renowned word associated with Christendom, second of course to Jesus Christ! At this point, as much as its popular, faith is still put on the back burner as we walk out this thing called 'Life'. I have been hired to be your Faith tour guide. In order to ride the 'Faith it to Make It" train, you must be willing to purchase a ticket, so you may see the different displays; scenarios; and views faith has to offer! Your ticket also includes personalized God moments designed to awaken, reinvigorate, and ignite your faith, so it will no longer lie dormant. As your tour guide, I will not only share my personal experiences and fight fear in your behalf, I will also prepare you for the areas/places you wish to take a closer look!

REFLECTION:

___

___

___

___

___

___

___

___

___

___

Prophetess Alicia L. Amis is an avid Teacher, a Robust Evangelist, and an Enthusiastic Submitted Prophet of the Lord. She is the founder of Called Out Global Outreach Ministry, a Prayer and Prophetic ministry focused on training, teaching, and helping one utilize tools to stabilize the total "man" naturally & Spiritually. Prophetess Alicia L. Amis is a Best-Selling Author and Founder/CEO of Never A-Mis Enterprises, LLC.

Social Media FB: CalledOutInternational **IG:** called_outministries

ACTIVATE YOUR FAITH

Dr. Derashay Zorn, Kingdom Strategist

"Thus also faith by itself, if it does not have works, is dead."

James 2:17

It's one thing to say you got faith, but it's a game changer when you can see your faith in action. Many people are looking to receive the promises of God with the expectation that it requires nothing of them. This mindset has caused many to leave this earth without receiving His promises. Inactive faith doesn't produce any fruit. James states it very well. *Faith without action is dead.* Saying you have faith isn't enough. It must be backed by a belief that will produce action. That's where your faith is ignited and activated to move toward the promise. This will cause you to engage in activities that align with your faith and produce the results of your faith. It's important that the activities you engage in steer you toward the destination of your expected end. Don't waste your time engaging in things that do not bring you closer to what you desire in your heart.

Entrepreneur Thought: Will the activities that you are producing bring forth the results you are expecting?

Entrepreneur Prayer: Dear God, I thank you for the measure of faith you gave me. Give me the wisdom and courage to operate in it, in Jesus' name, amen.

REFLECTION:

Kingdom Strategist, Blueprint Builder, and Spiritual Midwife, Dr. Derashay Zorn is an international business coach and best-selling author. She helps the faith-based community magnetize and monetize their influence and impact by creating profitable brands that develop long-lasting relationships with products and services their ideal client loves.

Discover how she can take your message and develop your next book, membership program, course, educational platform, coaching program, and more by visiting https://px.fyi/teawiththestrategist.

Social Media FB | IG: kingdom.strategist **Website:** www.derashay.com

WAIT ON HIM

Pastor Tamela Lucus

"But they that wait upon the LORD shall renew their strength; they shall mount up with wings as eagles; they shall run, and not be weary; and they shall walk, and not faint."

Isaiah 40:31 KJV

At the age of 20, I became an instant mom. Because my mother died and I had to raise my siblings. In addition, I was told by my doctor that I would never have children. But I didn't allow the doctor's report to hinder my belief. However, my trust had to be in the Lord. It's easy to tell others, "Hold on, everything is going to be alright." But the reality is our stomach is turning. Our heart is beating, and our head hurts. Sickness tries to come in because of anxiety. We are constantly telling ourselves we have to put our trust in God. We have to use the stop, drop, and roll method. Make yourself humble. Drop and cut everything down. Lay prostrate before him. Stay there until you hear from God. Then roll out His command with a spirit of obedience. When you wait on the Lord, He will renew your strength and give you the instructions and assurance to manifest His promise. Because I waited on the Lord and trusted in Him, I was able to deliver three children despite the doctor's report. If He can do it for me, I am positive He can do it for you. For nothing is impossible for our God.

REFLECTION:

International best-selling author, educational specialist, songwriter, and Psalmist Pastor Tamela Lucus is the host of Come Home, Stop Talking About It. She is a wife, a mother of nine, and a grandmother of seven.

Social Media FB: tamela.marie1 | **IG: @** doctat

LOYALTY IS A LIFESTYLE

Dr. Derashay Zorn, Kingdom Strategist

"O Lord God of Abraham, Isaac, and Israel, our fathers, keep this forever in the intent of the thoughts of the heart of Your people, and fix their heart toward You."

1 Chron. 29:18 NJKV

If God weighted your loyalty on a scale between Him and man, would your loyalty to God outweigh your loyalty unto man?

God is loyal. Therefore, we should be loyal people. We should be loyal to God in marriages, families, friendship, business, careers, and in all that we do. We fail to be loyal in other areas of our lives because of our neglect of loyalty to God. Loyalty flows from the top down. When we become loyal to God, it will not work to display loyalty in the other areas of our lives. When loyalty is a lifestyle, it infiltrates everything we do, and the results will bring forth an increase within our lives. Loyalty could have been a missing component to your level of increase. Let this year spring forth loyalty as a lifestyle so you can be successful in all you do.

Loyalty is a commitment to an ongoing relationship and to the attitude and behavior demanded by it. It is evident in human relationships and in the covenant relationship between God and his people.

Dear Lord, I thank you for a lifestyle of loyalty unto you, in Jesus' name, amen.

REFLECTION:

____

____

____

____

____

____

____

Kingdom Strategist, Blueprint Builder, and Spiritual Midwife, Dr. Derashay Zorn is an international business coach and best-selling author. She helps the faith based community magnetize and monetize their influence and impact by creating profitable brands that develop long-lasting relationships with products and services their ideal client loves.

Discover how she can take your message and develop your next book, membership program, course, educational platform, coaching program, and more by visiting https://px.fyi/teawiththestrategist.

Social Media FB | IG: kingdom.strategist **Website:** www.derashay.com

THE PRESENT (21ST CENTURY PARABLES)

Melissa Baines

Or do you not know that your body is a temple of the Holy Spirit within you, whom you have from God? You are not your own, 20 for you were bought with a price. So glorify God in your body.

1 Corinthians 6:19-20 ESV

As I began to wrap a present, I suddenly discovered I'd done so many things WRONG. For example, I thought the paper was shades of pink, but they were red. I thought I'd purchased two different types of wrapping paper. However, not one, but both of those rolls were transparent cellophane! Nevertheless, I took to meticulously wrapping my gift. I adjusted where I could, nipping and tucking the rest. Then, it occurred to me, this was much like the time and attention the father put into making us! My back began to hurt, and I even felt a tension headache begin to come upon me. I'm not at all trying to compare myself to our magnificent Lord. I'm kind of stuck for the time being in a mortal unfinished body, where He's still "wrapping"/completing the good work He's begun. However, I painstakingly (sounds kind of like Jesus on the cross for us) wanted to present the gift as immaculately as possible because of my love for my sister and friend, whom the gift was slated for. Please understand, this was not a gift for my own mom or my biological sister; least someone could say I let natural family ties guide my actions. No, this was a birthday gift for one of my sisters in Christ! Because I wanted to present it to her without spot or wrinkle, I took a little extra time. It wasn't perfect or even as pretty as I would have liked it to be, but what really mattered was what was on the inside! Right?

What's on the inside of your "wrapping"? Won't you let Him fix it up for final, and complete presentation?

REFLECTION:

____

____

____

____

____

____

Melissa, more familiarly known as Missy/Sis. Missy, considers herself as one The Lord is completing His Good Work in. Among her many Kingdom Assignments, her most meaningful and heartwarming are that of an adoptive and God mother, missionary, and exhorter. The Lord uses Missy strategically in diverse relationships and networking, where her faith is shared freely.

Social Media FB | Melissa (Missy) Baines

BE THE LIGHT

Rev. Rita M. Henderson

"Let your light so shine before men"

Matt. 5:14-16.

Going about the busy routines of our lives, we often find ourselves surviving instead of thriving. Believe in yourself and the fact that you were not put on this Earth to merely exist or survive – you have a purpose. As we step into adulthood, we start doing what we call "accepting the harsh reality." However, the only reality that exists in our life is the one we choose to believe. It all depends on us, and it all starts from us. We view everything from the filter of our own beliefs – once we correct our beliefs, all the other pieces fall into place.

Ultimately, the only thing that can keep us thriving is inner peace. True and absolute peace can be found only by becoming the light we were created to be. Only by playing what positive roles we can in the lives of our fellow beings will we be able to enjoy a tranquil and purposeful life. Whatever we give comes back to us. Working only and basically to serve our own cause will never let us be at peace with what we have – we will keep wanting and struggling for more.

Instead of trying to attain luxuries and powers solely for ourselves, let us try giving out what we can to others. What does not mean much or cost us much might be exactly what a fellow human being needs to enjoy a happy and healthy moment, day, or even life. Try giving what you want to receive – it will come back to you.

REFLECTION:

____

____

____

____

____

____

Reverend Rita Monique Henderson is a speaker, self-publishing coach, the CEO of Five-Fold Christian Publishing, LLC, and a three-time Amazon best-selling author.

Outside of the titles and accolades, Reverend Rita is a faith-fueled woman on a divine assignment to provide Christian ministers and leaders with the publishing strategies, guidance, and resources they need to turn their stories into influential, income-producing books that impact the world. She believes Your story can (and will) change lives. Visit aspiringchristianauthors.com, so she can show you how to publish and reach the masses.

Facebook: prophetesrita.henderson **IG:** @reverend_rita

Website: www.5foldpublishing.com

THIS THING CALLED LOVE

Evangelist Deborah Aguilera Aguilar

"Love never fails"

I Cor.13:4-8.

What is this thing called love, and why is it important for us to know and understand God's plan for marriage? For Jeremiah 29:11 says, "For I know the thoughts (plans) I have for you, saith the Lord. Thoughts of peace and not of evil to give you an expected end." Therefore, we must trust God completely. Know that if this is His Perfect will for you to be married, you will get married. Know that He has already prepared your mate for you with certainty. God will not give any bad thing to us.

If you truly desire to be a wife, prepare yourself to be a wife. Act like wife material now by setting and keeping your values and standards. No matter what he promises you, if you are not married to him, do not give him the benefits of a marriage partner. Give yourself more credit than that. Love yourself more. Learn to put value on the wonderful creation God made you to be.

Women of Value present yourself with value. Know that God has validated you, rather you be single or married. Through the validation of Jesus Christ, there is no need to look for validation from anyone. Look within the Love of God. Look at yourself in the eyes of Christ. God made you! He made you marvelously and wonderfully. You were made from the rib of man. We were not made from beneath his feet but from the rib that is on his side.

God has validated us and calls us daughters!

REFLECTION:

____

____

____

____

____

____

____

One day in October 2001, Evangelist Deborah Aguilera Aguilar found herself lost on a bridge in Jacksonville, Florida. After going around in circles about ten times, she began to panic. Then, she heard the voice of the Lord say, "I will give you the cities."

The Lord instructed her to minister to women from all walks of life. She was to show them love and encourage them not to give up on life. Evangelist Deborah has been called to serve women who are drug dependent, homeless, and lost in despair. In providing comfort and love, she would remind these women how much they are loved and valued by the Lord.

Social Media FB | pinesdeborah **Website:** www.womenofvalueministries.com

ARE YOU TIRED YET?

Minister Alinda Miller

"Now fear the LORD and serve him with all faithfulness…….. But as for me and my household, we will serve the LORD"

Joshua 24:14-15 NIV

We live our lives doing what pleases us. We go where we want to go, and we do what we want to do, but how many have sought God for guidance. We say we love God. We're followers of God, and we are His children. Some have said, "Lord I want to do your will!"

Let's look at our lives. How many have done or are still doing things because you want too? You spend money you weren't supposed to spend, took a job you knew wasn't for you, or smoke or drank, knowing you shouldn't. You even dated or messed around with someone you know wasn't meant for you and ate foods you weren't supposed to have. However, you made the choice to do what you wanted. What was the consequences? We don't want to be like the ancestors, doing what they wanted.

When you're obedient and choose who you will serve and follow, you will be blessed beyond measure. Don't let the day-to-day activities allow you to forget to seek the Lord in your choices and decisions. God is our Father; He is here to guide you and make sure no hurt, harm, or danger will happen to you. Seek the Lord and ask for guidance and instructions.

REFLECTION:

____

____

____

____

____

____

____

____

Minister Alinda Miller is a child of God who has served him from a young age. She is from Detroit, Michigan. From childhood, she has had a relationship with the Lord and as she grew, it became stronger. Prayer time with the Lord has always been her number one priority. She calls it "Talk Time" with the Lord. In early 2016 the Lord inspired her to share the prayers on media. The Lord has taken her to another level through her writing.

Minister Alinda holds a bachelor's degree, a master's degree, and continues to study. Alinda Miller is also a minister and chaplain.

Social Media FB | IG:@RefreshingMinistriesLLC

READY

Sharon P. Jones

"Watch therefore: for ye know not what hour your Lord doth come. But know this, that if the goodman of the house had known in what watch the thief would come, he would have watched, and would not have suffered his house to be broken up"

Matthew 24:42-43

Ready means to be in a suitable state for an activity, action, or situation; fully prepared (Google's English dictionary by Oxford Languages). As a Christian, we must stay in a state of preparedness so that we can effectively fight and overcome the tricks of the enemy. To stay in a ready position, we must not only read the Bible, but we must also do what it says. We are required to love God with all our heart, soul, and mind; we are also required to love our neighbors to the degree that we love ourselves. The love is a commandment, not an option. Love is a powerful weapon that aids us as Christians as we walk through our day-to-day lives. Our walk, talk, and actions as Christians are a preached word, and the Bible reminds us we are to be always ready, in season and out of season. Let's commit to prepare so we can be ready.

REFLECTION:

Sharon P. Jones is an international best-selling author, certified life coach and entrepreneur. She is a wife and mother who lives in Atlanta where she serves in ministry with her husband.

Social Media FB | IG: @wotflglobal; **Facebook:** Sharon Jones Author

MONEY ISN'T EVIL

Dr. Derashay Zorn, Kingdom Strategist

"For the love of money is a root of all kinds of evil, for which some have strayed from the faith in their greediness, and pierced themselves through with many sorrows. "

1 Tim. 6:10 NKJV

Money doesn't have the ability to do anything evil. However, those who possess it can have the ability to do good or evil. Many people in the faith-based communities have found themselves living beneath God's desire for His people because a narrative has been created that money is evil. In fact, the love of money is the root of all of it. When people love money, they will do whatever it takes to possess it because money has become their master. Therefore, instead of running away from the wealth that God has called you to have, we must embrace it. After embracing it, we must make a conscious decision that money will not become our master. It will not be something that drives us. Instead, it will be something that is attracted to us. There is a difference between driven and attracted. When you are driven by something, you are under its control, and you are chasing after it. On the other hand, when something is attracted to you, it is subject to you, and it chases after you.

Dear God, I thank you that I attract wealth, and I don't chase it. I praise you because I will never be a slave or servant to money, in the name of Jesus, amen.

REFLECTION:

____
____
____
____
____
____
____

Kingdom Strategist, Blueprint Builder, and Spiritual Midwife, Dr. Derashay Zorn is an international business coach and best-selling author. She helps the faith-based community magnetize and monetize their influence and impact by creating profitable brands that develop long-lasting relationships with products and services their ideal client loves.

Discover how she can take your message and develop your next book, membership program, course, educational platform, coaching program, and more by visiting https://px.fyi/teawiththestrategist.

Social Media FB | IG: kingdom.strategist **Website:** www.derashay.com

CHANGE IS WAITING

Jeauniné S. Boyce

"And be not conformed to this world: but be ye transformed by the renewing of your mind, that ye may prove what is that good, and acceptable, and perfect, will of God."

Romans 12:2

The meaning of change is to make (someone or something) different, alter, or modify. It can be extremely difficult to make changes AND to maintain them, especially the ones that are comfortable! We'll talk and/or complain about changes, but things remain the same! Change is a verb.... it's an action word! Action means the fact or process of doing something, typically to achieve an aim. Therefore, for things to change, YOU have work to do!!!!! Get a journal and make a list of all the things you want to change! Be realistic and pick one! Write down WHY it needs to be changed. Be realistic and embrace all that comes with it (positive and negative)! Next, write HOW you can change it. Be realistic and prepare for self-accountability and discipline! You'll NEED both! The journal will be your guide to start the process AND to maintain the process! Make your journal a daily pleasure! It gives you a chance to re-read, adjust, check off what you've accomplished and prepare for what's next. However, remember, this process demands discipline and self-accountability! If you want change, CHANGE! #itstartswithYOU

REFLECTION:

Jeauniné S. Boyce is the founder of Heart Conversations with Jeauniné, LLC. She is a certified life coach, daughter, sister, mother, and grandmother.

Instagram: Conversations_with_Jeaunine

THE RIGHT TO HEAL

Denise M. Walker

"O God, You are my God, I shall seek you earnestly; my soul thirsts for You, my flesh yearns for You, in a dry and weary land where there is no water"
Psalm 63:1 NASB.

It is God's will that we heal. There are some things that cause us to become much like King David in Psalm 63 - tired, fatigued, weary, or barren.

Many of us may endure struggles that steal our God-given identity, which in turn causes our weariness or barrenness. We grow tired of running from the source of our pain. We grow weary attempting to cover it all up by perfecting our appearance, seeking acceptance from others, chasing success, and so much more.

As we seek these things, we don't recognize we are attempting to substitute God's rest for our soul with the temporal. Most of all, we become stagnant, failing to move in God's purpose. Therefore, we must seek the living God earnestly for the quenching of our soul's thirst. We must allow God to heal us and make us whole in Him, so we are not left longing and wondering in a spiritual wilderness once again, when the temporal things are all gone.

Come forth and be made whole in Christ.

REFLECTION:

Denise M. Walker is a minister, author, copy editor, writing coach, podcaster, educator, speaker, and workshop host. Denise has authored eight books, co-authored several anthologies, and has written many devotionals for the Hope-in-Christ website. She is the founder of Hope-in-Christ Ministries, Inc. and is the CEO of Armor of Hope Writing & Publishing Services, LLC.

Social Media FB | IG: @authordenisemwalker

Website: www.denisemwalker.com

TROUBLED TIMES!

Evangelist Vickie Chiney-Smith

"For in the time of trouble he shall hide me in his pavilion: in the secret of his tabernacle shall he hide me; he shall set me up upon a rock"

Psalm 27:5

Man that is born of a woman is of few days, and full of trouble (Job 14:1). There is a growth process in the scheme of life, where you develop from stage to stage. You start out as a baby born to a man and woman who take care of you because you're not capable of taking care of yourself. Your parents are responsible for your well-being and safety. The mother starts taking care of you in the womb, and the father joins in after birth. They protect you from troubles that you are not even aware of.

Next, you go through a learning stage that teaches you basic survival and human interaction. You develop an opinion as you become aware of trouble and start applying what you have been taught to learn how to manage it. Your parents rescue and shield you until you become of age to fend for yourself. Sometimes, they must stand down and let you have the experience on your own to learn the lesson. Because of Adam and Eve, man is born a slave to sin and serves Satan. Christ came and bought salvation and deliverance from sin. You are born again in the spirit when you receive it. God becomes your Father, and you become His servant. Jesus shows you how to cope with trouble! There are tests and trials that no one can protect you from but God. As you serve Him, He puts up a shield of protection all around you and keeps you safe and close to him.

REFLECTION:

____

____

____

____

____

____

____

____

Evangelist Vickie Chiney-Smith (EVCS) is a servant of God, dedicated to Kingdom building. She hosts the MID-DAY weekly Bible Study every Tuesday @ 2pm CST on Divine Order Restoration Ministries FB, Dr. Derashay Zorn, Kingdom Strategist, founder. EVCS goes by "The Praise Raiser." Her motto is: "RAISE THE PRAISE (RTP)! ALRIGHT!

Social Media FB: RTPEVCS **Website:** http://www.thepraiseraiser.com

ATTITUDE IS EVERYTHING!

Wakeitha Cunningham

"Trust in the Lord with all your heart, and do not lean on your own understanding."

Proverb 3:5

What does attitude is everything mean?

In my opinion, my attitude is one thing I have control over as a human being. A personal mission of mine is to work on my attitude each day! The more I work on it, it works on me! My motto is "My peace is my priority!" I could choose to focus on the negative or the problems in my life but choosing to have a positive attitude means everything. Having a positive attitude allows me to move forward in my purpose!

How to keep a positive attitude:

1. Think big – God's vision is bigger than mine!
2. Think other people – Include others in the plan!
3. Think continual growth – Keep improving!
4. Think victory – Be victorious!
5. Think servanthood – Serve and add value to people!

What are 5 things you can do to improve your attitude?

REFLECTION:

____

____

____

____

____

____

____

Wakeitha Cunningham is a passion pursuer coach, international best-selling author, speaker, a mother of two, and an influential woman of God on a mission to be a light to God's people. She has a passion for helping others pursue their passions and walk in their God given purpose. Wakeitha encourages others to focus on their passions instead of their problems and pain.

Email: coachwcunningham@gmail.com

THE POWER IN THE DESERT

Dr. Derashay Zorn, Kingdom Strategist

"Therefore, I am now going to allure her; I will lead her into the desert and speak tenderly to her"

Hosea 2:14.

The desert is only to get your attention so the Lord can speak tenderly unto your heart. He has lured you into the desert because, in the field, you were too distracted from hearing His voice. While in the desert (your dry places, your lack), don't focus or put your attention on the desert. Give yourself attentively unto the Lord. He desires to speak unto you His plans of promise, of purpose, of destiny.

Know, beloved that your desert experience is not a setback for you but a setup to propel you in my glory says the Lord. As you are attentive to my voice, streams of living water are going to begin to flow within the desert. As you, have an ear to hear My Spirit, your places of barrenness will begin to flourish. Mountains are going to be laid flat on your behalf and pathways developed just for you. This will be for the enlargement of your dwelling.

Entrepreneur Thought: Don't complain in the drought. Just listen for the word of the Lord.

Entrepreneur Prayer: *Lord, I thank you for luring me into the desert, so I can hear from you without distraction. May my soul remain silent so it will not murmur, and may my heart and eyes be attentive to every word you utter, in Jesus' name, amen.*

REFLECTION:

____

____

____

____

____

____

Kingdom Strategist, Blueprint Builder, and Spiritual Midwife, Dr. Derashay Zorn is an international business coach and best-selling author. She helps the faith-based community magnetize and monetize their influence and impact by creating profitable brands that develop long-lasting relationships with products and services their ideal client loves.

Discover how she can take your message and develop your next book, membership program, course, educational platform, coaching program, and more by visiting https://px.fyi/teawiththestrategist.

Social Media FB | IG: kingdom.strategist **Website:** www.derashay.com

POWER IN YOUR PAIN

Vanetta Anderson

"But he said to me, 'My grace is sufficient for you, for my power is made perfect in weakness." Therefore I will boast all the more gladly about my weaknesses, so that Christ's power may rest on me"

2 Cor 12:9.

For 40 years I was wandering in the wilderness of life, lost with no purpose or direction. To the outside world, I was considered accomplished. Wife, mother, and MBA were all the markers that indicated "success." On the inside, I was broken. The pain and trauma of my childhood and the depressive anxiety-filled episodes led me to a perpetual state of life-paralysis.

It is in our darkest hour and our weakest state, that God is most powerful. When we are afraid, He can provide a peace beyond our understanding. When the pains of life become all-encompassing, He will lift you up and guide you toward His purpose for your life, a purpose so divine it will change the trajectory of other people's lives.

Release your pain and trust God with the results. The light that shines within will lead you out of the dark wilderness and into a season filled with Kingdom purpose.

REFLECTION:

Vanetta Anderson is a real estate agent/entrepreneur. She is passionate about helping people create the life they envision through spiritual, mental, and financial wellness.

Social Media FB: vanetta.l.anderson | **IG** the.vanderson.group

Website: www.liveworkplayregroup.com/agents/staff

CHARACTER DEVELOPMENT

Nico Olivia

"And let us consider how to stir up one another to love and good works."

Heb. 10:24 (ESV)

Jealousy can manifest in various forms, even in the form of someone allegedly supporting you. Yet, there exists deep-seated ill feelings towards you.

Firstly, they may have feelings to compete. Then, there is a shift to feelings for your failure and demise. This is found in many streams of life, from the family dynamic to the workplace and sadly ministry.

Besides hidden sexual sin that would create kinks in your armor, not dealing with inward character traits like insecurity, low self-esteem, low self-worth, lack of self-love, pride, ego and personal weaknesses and inadequacies are a recipe for disaster in your walk and life with God. Undealt with character will seep through your spirit man and manifest into the natural world.

The anointing without having its bedrock on a solid, well-built, established, mature character will have no promise of longevity (meteoric rise).

You may be outwardly displaying power, yet inwardly dying a slow, agonizing death, because you chose to compete rather than function in your unique, innate capacity! A spirit of jealousy and competition can cause you to operate outside of your designated mandate, thus having devastating repercussions.

Learn and extract from others but never mimic. Be authentic. Invest time in honing your skills. Above all, develop CHARACTER, which will sustain you, especially in the difficult times.

REFLECTION:

____

____

____

____

____

____

Nico Olivia is the founder and creative director of multimedia and brand communication company - Eminence. Her expertise includes copywriting and marketing strategist for companies in the Marketing and Advertising industry.

As a Kingdom scribe who carries an Apostolic Prophetic / Intercessory mantle, she specializes in counselling, coaching, business coaching, business administration, training, self-development, and personal mastery, both in the Kingdom and secular environment.

Social Media FB: nico.o.favour **| IG:** iam_nicoolivia

EXPERIENCE GOD THE FATHER

William Rodgers

"The Lord hath appeared of old unto me, saying, Yeah I have loved thee with an everlasting love: therefore, with lovingkindness have I drawn thee."

Jeremiah 31: 3 KJV

God has been drawing many in this hour because He loves us, His people, and He wants to be our father. Many men have found it difficult to receive God's love as a father because of their experience with their earthly fathers. Many have experienced abandonment, rejection, and disappointments of their earthly father and have begun to look at God like man. God has called many. However, because of this experience, they are stagnant. I could never truly experience the love of God because of my mindset of a father's love. God loves each of us, but we must develop a true relationship with Christ through a life of prayer, worship, and studying His word. God's love as a father is to teach men His love so they can display it in the earth. Where are the earthly fathers today? God's spirit is in man to teach him His ways. The earth needs the fathers love more than ever before. Many are walking in their purpose today but lack the father's love in fighting for His standards in the earth. God is fighting for each of us, and it's time we fight for Him. As God is drawing you to be your Father, accept His love and learn His ways. Let Him be a father to you so you can be a father to many.

REFLECTION:

____

____

____

____

____

____

____

____

Ordained Elder and teacher, Prophet William Rodgers is a man chasing after the heart of God. He is no stranger to adversity. The mighty call on his life has made him a target of the adversary. He has tried to take him out repeatedly. His life of addiction has caused him to seek the Lord for healing and deliverance and to receive the love of the father. He currently resides in Asheville, North Carolina and is the pastor of His Grace Is Sufficient Ministries.

Social Media FB | IG: William Ben Rodgers

TAP INTO YOUR WEALTH

Dr. Derashay Zorn, Kingdom Strategist

"And you shall remember the Lord your God, for it is He who gives you power to get wealth, that He may establish His covenant which He swore to your fathers, as it is this day."

Deut. 8:18 NKJV

Did you know there is wealth inside of you awaiting to emerge? The Bible tells us God has given us the power to generate wealth. This would mean that we have the ability to produce it. People desire wealth but fail to tap into what God has given them to generate it. To tap into this power or ability, you must understand what God has called you to do.

If you are pondering on the ability God has given you, begin with what you are naturally good at doing. What are the things people ask you to do the most, and what are you passionate about that you would do for free? Answering these questions for yourself will put you on the path of knowing exactly the ability God has given you. Your next step is to determine ways you can package it and put it into the marketplace. Notice, I said ways because to get to the wealth, your message or ability will need to be packaged for different platforms. This is so your wealth streams are diversified. Give yourself a try. Start with packaging your superpower onto one platform. Then, give yourself permission to grow from there.

REFLECTION:

____

____

____

____

____

____

____

____

Kingdom Strategist, Blueprint Builder, and Spiritual Midwife, Dr. Derashay Zorn is an international business coach and best-selling author. She helps the faith-based community magnetize and monetize their influence and impact by creating profitable brands that develop long-lasting relationships with products and services their ideal client loves.

Discover how she can take your message and develop your next book, membership program, course, educational platform, coaching program, and more by visiting https://px.fyi/teawiththestrategist.

Social Media FB | IG: kingdom.strategist **Website:** www.derashay.com

DISCOVERING YOUR IDENTITY

Lillian Tinsley

"For we are his workmanship, created in Christ Jesus unto good works, which God hath before ordained that we should walk in them."

Ephesians 2:10

It is natural to desire relationship. Healthy relationships are not formed when individuals don't know their true identity in Christ. They will devalue themselves and allow others to do the same. We are children of God. This happens when we cannot embrace sonship and take on the spirit of an orphan. Trauma in our upbringing and lives will cause us to hold on to things or individuals who are toxic. The longer we stay connected to them we begin to lose value in ourselves because we want that person to desperately see our worth. When these types of connections evolve, it is impossible for them to evolve in a healthy manner, whether it is a work relationship, a business partnership, friendship, or marriage. We must understand that we are God's masterpiece. We are a gift and precious to God. We must do the work to untie the soul and allow God to heal and deliver us so we will see ourselves as a gift and not allow any connection that does not value the gift we are.

REFLECTION:

____

____

____

____

____

____

____

____

Minister Lillian Jackson Tinsley is a native of Lakeland, Florida. She is a Counselor, Teacher, Mentor, Motivational Speaker, Psalmist, and Liturgical Dancer. Lillian is dedicated to serving the people of God. One of her greatest passions is to use her God-given abilities to snatch people out of the fire of hopelessness, insecurities, depression, and despair. She birthed Healing Heart's Personal Touch Ministries out of the pain and devastation of surviving rape and domestic violence. Lillian is the mother of two beautiful daughters, two grandchildren, and mother to many young adults that pursue excellence and wholeness in mind, body, and spirit. Ms. Tinsley has a MA degree in Mental Health and Marriage & Family Counseling from Webster University.

Social Media FB: | @ lillian.tinsley **IG:** lil_lillian01

GOD IS OUR REFUGE

Sharon Dawson-McElveen

"If it had not been for the Lord who was on our side, let Israel now say."
Psalm 124:1

Today, I have so much to be thankful for. During my tender years as a young adult, I struggled with wanting to fit in. But there was something different about me. Then one day it happened. Addiction became my portion. As I struggled to overcome the entanglement and spirit of substance use, I would remember the words from my grandmother; "Jesus loves you. Trust him and He will bring you through."

You may not have an addiction, but there might be something that grips you with an un-assurance. Just as David encourages the Israelites, he encourages us too, "If it had not been for the Lord who was on our side."

We can ponder this for a moment and make it personal. If it had not been for the Lord who was and still is on my side, I would not be here today. We have a savior who created us to be different and for his purpose.

As we can see, God will protect us and keep us. Although we may go through the storms and roaring rivers, we will not be overtaken. Today, keep in mind that your Savior is with you, and He is on your side always.

REFLECTION:

___

Born and raised in New York City, Sharon felt a calling on her life as a young girl. Pastor Sharon holds a master's degree in Pastoral Care and Christian Counseling. She is the founder of Rose of Sharon Street Outreach Ministries, LLC. She serves as the Pastor over the outreach ministries at her church, where she leads her team in serving the community and those under bridges.

Social Media FB: Sharon Dawson McElveen

PLAN TO PROFIT

Dr. Derashay Zorn, Kingdom Strategist

"The plans of the diligent lead to profit as surely as haste leads to poverty."

Proverbs 21:5 NKJV

Every business or individual with a product or service has the capacity to generate profits because they solve a problem within the world. However, to obtain the profits, one must plan for them. If you fail to plan, how are you going to produce profits with what you got. Then you have officially plan to fail in making profits with it.

To make a substantial amount of profit, we must plan for it. When you are planning for your profit, you must start with how much money you desire to make for the year. Then, you must determine what products or services you are going to use to generate the income. After that, you move to determining how many products and /or services you need to sale to hit your targeted profit goal. Once those numbers are determined, you should break down the sale numbers by quarters, months, weeks, and days. This will break down your profit plan into smaller quantities that equal to your goal for the year. Upon completion of finding out how many of which products and/or services you need to sale daily, it's time to implement the plan. Now, there are 3 other P's you will need to consider. They are the people (who's your target audience?), the platforms (where are you promoting, where will they purchase, and how will it be delivered?), and the payments (how are they going to pay you?)

REFLECTION:

____

____

____

____

____

____

____

Kingdom Strategist, Blueprint Builder, and Spiritual Midwife, Dr. Derashay Zorn is an international business coach and best-selling author. She helps the faith-based community magnetize and monetize their influence and impact by creating profitable brands that develop long-lasting relationships with products and services their ideal client loves.

Discover how she can take your message and develop your next book, membership program, course, educational platform, coaching program, and more by visiting https://px.fyi/teawiththestrategist.

Social Media FB | IG: kingdom.strategist **Website:** www.derashay.com

PROTECT YOUR GIFT

Lillian Tinsley

"Neglect not the gift that is in thee"

1 Timothy 4:14

To be given a gift and not cultivate, guard, nurture, and protect it is telling God we don't appreciate the gift that He's given. It's not always the devil blocking our gifts. At times, it is our unwillingness to change, surrender, and submit to the will of God in our lives. Mismanagement of the gift will cause a delay or God to move His hand off a situation. It will take discipline, sacrifice, and a surrender of your will to handle your gift maturely.

Transparent moment: I have not always valued myself, and I allowed individuals to connect to me that did not value me either nor did they have my best interest in mind. After 22 years of concealing my story out of fear of disrupting what appeared to be a community of love, family, and friendship, I could no longer remain silent, so I spoke. As a result of my honest introspection and transparency, the mask came off and liberated me to discover my authentic self. Through my transparency came revelation of healing, areas of personal deliverance needed, and the awareness of my unique purpose, which is healing hearts and an appreciation for God's grace and love towards me. As I shared my story, my scars empowered me to no longer view myself as a victim but as a victor.

REFLECTION:

____

____

____

____

____

____

____

Minister Lillian Jackson Tinsley is a native of Lakeland, Florida. She is a Counselor, Teacher, Mentor, Motivational Speaker, Psalmist, and Liturgical Dancer. Lillian is dedicated to serving the people of God. One of her greatest passions is to use her God-given abilities to snatch people out of the fire of hopelessness, insecurities, depression, and despair. She birthed Healing Heart's Personal Touch Ministries out of the pain and devastation of surviving rape and domestic violence. Lillian is the mother of two beautiful daughters, two grandchildren, and mother to many young adults that pursue excellence and wholeness in mind, body, and spirit. Ms. Tinsley has a MA degree in Mental Health and Marriage & Family Counseling from Webster University.

Social Media FB: | @ lillian.tinsley **IG:** lil_lillian01

THE EVIL TWIN

Evangelist Vickie Chiney-Smith

"I find then a law, that, when I would do good, evil is present with me"

Rom. 7:21

The flesh verses the Spirit is an age-old war that has been going on since the beginning of time. The theme of the battle between evil and good is Satan's disobedience pitted against God's righteousness. Satan already knows that he can't win, but he uses his power to wage war and rob God of the souls that belong to Him. Why? It is because Satan is evil. There are others like him, whom he is seeks to recruit. They too will share his punishment in the eternal lake of fire. On the other hand, those who love God and follow after His righteousness will be on the right side of the fence and receive the blessings on earth and the eternal reward of being with God in heaven.

In Romans 6 and 7, Paul teaches the principles of sin and death verses life in Christ first because you can't be held accountable for what you don't know. However, once you learn, you are commanded to walk therein. Who you love is who you obey and follow after. The children of God will live unto Him and follow Christ. Satan's children live unto Him and follow the flesh. If you're pure at heart, God is your Father, and His will shall be done. If you're wicked, Satan is your father, and you will do his works. *Know ye not, that to whom ye yield yourselves servants to obey, his servants ye are to whom ye obey; whether of sin unto death, or of obedience unto righteousness (Rom. 6:16).*

REFLECTION:

____

____

____

____

____

____

____

____

Evangelist Vickie Chiney-Smith (EVCS) is a servant of God, dedicated to Kingdom building. She hosts the MID-DAY weekly Bible Study every Tuesday @ 2pm CST on Divine Order Restoration Ministries FB, Dr. Derashay Zorn, Kingdom Strategist, founder. EVCS goes by "The Praise Raiser." Her motto is: "RAISE THE PRAISE (RTP)! ALRIGHT!

Social Media FB: RTPEVCS **Website:** http://www.thepraiseraiser.com

REFUSE TO LOSE

Dr. Derashay Zorn, Kingdom Strategist

"No, in all these things we are more than conquerors through him who loved us."

Romans 8:37

I know there is a winner in you, even if you feel defeated and tired. This is the place where you allow God to strengthen you for the victory. In the book of Romans, Paul informed us that we are more than conquers in all things. Therefore, no matter what is coming up against us, we shall prevail in victory. He further gives us the strategy on how the victory is going to happen. It's important we don't overlook how we will triumph over our situation. The Apostle Paul says it's going to happen through Him who loves us. Hold up. Wait a minute. Without God, we cannot be victorious. He has the strategic plan to conquer our foes. It's time to refuse to lose and get in God's battle plan for our fixed victory.

I declare it's your winning season for all those who would trust in the Lord. Don't get caught up in who or what's fighting up against you. It's a time of focusing on God almighty, for He is bigger than your pain, struggles, disappointments, situations, and circumstances. He is going to strategically guide you to triumph. There is not one thing He will not give you the power to overcome and conquer. Be still, and you shall see the salvation of the Lord, in the name of Jesus, amen.

REFLECTION:

____

____

____

____

____

____

____

Kingdom Strategist, Blueprint Builder, and Spiritual Midwife, Dr. Derashay Zorn is an international business coach and best-selling author. She helps the faith-based community magnetize and monetize their influence and impact by creating profitable brands that develop long-lasting relationships with products and services their ideal client loves.

Discover how she can take your message and develop your next book, membership program, course, educational platform, coaching program, and more by visiting https://px.fyi/teawiththestrategist.

Social Media FB | IG: kingdom.strategist **Website:** www.derashay.com

YOU ARE MY GOD

Nichole Flowers

"all things work together for good to them that love God"

Romans 8:28

In the midst of our busy day to day activities, we tend to get lost in all of the things tugging for our attention. The kids, spouse or significant other, and our jobs all require so much of us.

Has your everyday activities ever turned into something bigger than what they needed to be? I can admit I have been overwhelmed by all the demands of my everyday life. I have even allowed those things to pull me away from God himself. If only I had decided to turn my focus towards God and away from those things, my days would have gone smoother. God wants to go before you in every area of your life and work it out on your behalf.

Today...don't allow ANYTHING to become bigger than your God.

REFLECTION:

___

___

___

___

___

___

___

___

___

___

Nichole Flowers is first and foremost a child of God! She operates in the gift of teaching in a public school setting in Indianapolis, Indiana.

She is a school mom to 25 boys and girls and the biological mother of 1 amazing son. She is also a proud member of Alpha Omega Chi Sorority Incorporated.

Social Media FB | nichole.flowers

POSITION FOR THE OFFENSE

Dr. Cecilia Jackson

"I will go and fight him." David said, "I take care of my father's sheep. Any time a lion or a bear carries off a lamb, I go after it, attack it, and rescue the lamb"

1Sa 17:32-35 (GNB).

This is the season in your life to come off the defensive line, get on the offensive line, and GO FORWARD!!

Defensive players function to stop the offensive player from being successful. In a football game, defensive players try to hold back the progress of the offensive line and attempts to prohibit their forward movement down the field.

The primary function of the offensive player is to move the ball down the field by either running with it or passing it to another offensive runner. Offensive players are intelligent and tough. They push the defensive players backward and make way for the ball carrier to pass. They are the strength and backbone of any team. To be offensive means YOU do something. Make the first aggressive move forward; the Lord is with you.

It is your season to advance forward to your next dimension, fulfilling desire, and purpose. Know that what you are passionate about is typically connected to your purpose, your happiness, your ministry, your God-intended mate, and your peace in an environment of chaos and turmoil. Get on the offensive line. Go Forward!

REFLECTION:

____

____

____

____

____

____

____

____

Dr. Cecilia Jackson is an official delegate of the United Nations for the Cause of Women. She has authored 36 professional publications. She is the founder and Co-Provost of the "I AM" College of Ministry. Dr. Cecilia is also the founder of Seasoned Anointed Oil for Regional Women in Leadership, a state certified educator, radio show host, and spiritual mid-wife. Email: drcjackson3712@gmail.com

Social Media FB | IG: I AM Productions Publishing

Website: iamfellowshipministries.net

LIKE A FLOOD

Melissa Baines

"So they came up to Baalperazim; and David smote them there. Then David said, God hath broken in upon mine enemies by mine hand like the breaking forth of waters: therefore they called the name of that place Baalperazim."

1 Chronicles 14:11

I studied 1 Chronicles 14:11, "God has broken through to my enemies LIKE THE BURSTING FORTH OF WATER."

Holy Spirit brought Isaiah 59:19 to mind, "So shall they fear the name of the Lord from the West and His Glory from the rising of the sun. When the enemy comes in LIKE A FLOOD, the Spirit of the Lord shall lift up a standard against him."

There have been questions whether it should be read, "... when the enemy comes in like a flood..." (as it is printed in most text) or "...when the enemy comes in, like a flood, the Lord shall lift up a standard..." I am convinced God's Word confirms itself! Further, 1 Chronicles 14 states that the place was named, Baal-Perazim, "God of The Breakthrough!" He is truly the God of our breakthrough, favor, healing, opportunity, knowledge, wisdom, and more!

Prayer: Thank You for meeting with me, Lord, and for visitation. Amen!

REFLECTION:

Melissa, more familiarly known as Missy/Sis. Missy, considers herself as one The Lord is completing His Good Work in. Among her many Kingdom Assignments, her most meaningful and heartwarming are that of an adoptive and God mother, missionary, and exhorter. The Lord uses Missy strategically in diverse relationships and networking, where her faith is shared freely.

Social Media FB | Melissa (Missy) Baines

MAKE A LASTING MARK

Dr. Derashay Zorn, Kingdom Strategist

"Now go, write it before them on a tablet, And note it on a scroll, That it may be for time to come, Forever and ever:

Isaiah 30:8 NKJV

Wouldn't it be great to leave something that will stand as a testament of the goodness of God in your life forever? God instructed Isaiah to write down the account of Israel's actions and what He was going to do so it would be an everlasting witness. In addition, God told the Israelites to write about the things He had done for them. He instructed them to write His commands on the doorpost, the gates, their hearts, hang them around their necks, and so forth. He was only saying, "If it's in a book, it could be passed down for generations to come." God desires you to leave a lasting mark by writing your story in a book so it can be passed down for generations. That serves as a tool to help others understand and know the power of God, trust in God, and obtain His promises. Has God allowed you to overcome anything? Has God given you a talent others can learn from or utilize? Then, let's get the book written so you can make an everlasting mark on the earth. Once you have written it, there are several ways you can leverage it to generate multiple streams of income. Just like the servant in the book of Luke chapter 19 multiplied their talents ten times, so can you.

Entrepreneur Thoughts: What has God done in your life? What talents have you been given to help somebody today?

Entrepreneur Prayer: *Father, give me the wisdom to write books of my testimony and talents as a tool to help others forever, in Jesus' name, amen.*

REFLECTION:

____

____

____

____

Kingdom Strategist, Blueprint Builder, and Spiritual Midwife, Dr. Derashay Zorn is an international business coach and best-selling author. She helps the faith-based community magnetize and monetize their influence and impact by creating profitable brands that develop long-lasting relationships with products and services their ideal client loves.

Discover how she can take your message and develop your next book, membership program, course, educational platform, coaching program, and more by visiting https://px.fyi/teawiththestrategist.

Social Media FB | IG: kingdom.strategist **Website:** www.derashay.com

REMEMBER YOUR ALTARS

Dr. Dawn L. Cooper

"Israel came over this Jordan on dry land."

Joshua 4:22

Have you ever experienced being blessed by God? Not your everyday blessings, but profound, miraculous, faith-building blessings. Perhaps God allowed you to buy a home you never thought you would own, a car you never imagined having, or he opened the door to a job or promotion. You were so excited and overjoyed. However, when God presented you with a task that you thought was too big, you became fearful, defeated, and deflated.

Joshua instructed the twelve tribes to build an altar of twelve stones, to serve as a reminder that God allowed them to cross over the Jordan River into the Promised Land. This would serve as a forever reminder that God will deliver His people and stay true to His promises.

Today, our alters are not physical but spiritual. It is vital to our walk with God to build altars in our heart to serve as reminders that increase our faith. Knowing if God did it for you in the past, He will do it for you again. Now, walk in your victory today!

REFLECTION:

Dr. Dawn L. Cooper is an international best-selling author who resides in Indianapolis, Indiana. She is called by God to deliver biblical principles that build the Kingdom of God on Earth. Dr. Cooper is the mother of six and the grandmother of 12.

Social Media FB: @dlcooperauthor **Website:** www.dlcooperauthor.com

AIM

Sharon P. Jones

"I press toward the mark for the prize of the high calling of God in Christ Jesus."

Philippians 3:14

Aim means to point or direct (a weapon or camera) at a target. When I decide to do something, it seems anything and everything happens to throw me off course. Life happens and everyone needs me for something or needs me to be somewhere. I know I'm not the only one this happens to.

When this happens, it's important to remain focused on the target (goal). There are situations or circumstances that are distractions. Learn to recognize when they arise and make the decision whether to address them accordingly. Be intentional about staying committed to the tasks associated with achieving a specific goal.

When aiming at the target, it's important for the vision to be clear, and make sure there is no debris or any other particles, or distractions blocking the target. The race is not given to the swift or the strongest but to the one who endures to the end. Let's commit to be focused on completing goals. Stay focused on what God has purposed you to do.

REFLECTION:

Sharon P. Jones is an international best-selling author, certified life coach and entrepreneur. She is a wife and mother who lives in Atlanta where she serves in ministry with her husband.

Social Media FB | IG: @wotflglobal**; Facebook:** Sharon Jones Author

ENCOURAGEMENT FOR YOUR ANOINTING AND LIFE ASSIGNMENT

Dr. Cecilia Jackson

"The sovereign LORD has filled me with his Spirit and has sent me to bring good news to the poor, to heal the broken-hearted, to announce release to captives and freedom to those bound and to proclaim the time has come when the LORD"

Isa 61:1-4

The ANOINTING is the triumphant power of God living and flowing through you to do what he assigned you to do on earth.

1) Your assignment was determined by the will of God, not your perfection. Do not be fearful to function but know you are a work in progress who he will continue to perfect.
2) The anointing in your life increases proportionate to your dependence on God, which comes from your continued surrender to His mind, will, word, and spirit.
3) Any destructive act against the anointing in you is forbidden by God, and He will deal with any violators of His rule. Cease from any worry about people who have not done well by you.
4) Your respect for the anointing in others will increase the blessing of God upon your life.
5) The anointing upon your life will attract and repel others. Understand those who always please people, typically do not always please the Lord.

REFLECTION:

____
____
____
____
____
____
____
____

Dr. Cecilia Jackson is: 1) Official Delegate of the United Nations for the Cause of Women 2) Author of 36 professional publications 3) Founder and Co-Provost of the "I AM" College of Ministry 4) Founder of Seasoned Anointed Oil for Regional Women in Leadership 5) State Certified Educator 6) Radio Show 7) spiritual Mid-wife Email: drcjackson3712@gmail.com

Social Media FB | IG: I AM Productions Publishing
Website: iamfellowshipministries.net

GOD DESIGNED YOU TO PROSPER

Dr. Derashay Zorn, Kingdom Strategist

"For I know the plans I have for you," declares the Lord, "plans to prosper you and not to harm you, plans to give you hope and a future."

Jer. 29:11 NKJV

It is such a wonderful feeling to know that God has designed us to prosper. The fact that He has declared it in His plans for our lives is an indicator that it is important to Him. The beauty is that He expects prosperity in every area of our lives -- mentally, emotionally, physically, financially, and spiritually. Obtaining the level of prosperity He desires is within our transformation. Many people don't acquire the wealth that God craves for our lives because we are too focused on the external prosperity, and it prohibits us from truly reaching it. God talks about it quite a bit in His word because He is so fixed on us having it. He said, "Everything we touch shall prosper. Prosperity shall come to you. You will live and prosper. I will make you prosper." There are so many more scriptures that reference it. I want to be clear that each one of the prosperity statements comes with conditions that must be met. However, just like anything else, if you desire the benefits, you will meet the expectations. To prosper in every area of our lives, we must come into alignment with God's word. He has spoken that His word will not come back unto Him void, but it shall accomplish that which He shall, and it shall prosper in the things He sent it.

REFLECTION:

Kingdom Strategist, Blueprint Builder, and Spiritual Midwife, Dr. Derashay Zorn is an international business coach and best-selling author. She helps the faith-based community magnetize and monetize their influence and impact by creating profitable brands that develop long-lasting relationships with products and services their ideal client loves.

Discover how she can take your message and develop your next book, membership program, course, educational platform, coaching program, and more by visiting https://px.fyi/teawiththestrategist.

Social Media FB | IG: kingdom.strategist **Website:** www.derashay.com

"ME TIME" MATTERS!

Wakeitha Cunningham

> *"Beloved, I pray that you may prosper in all things and be in health."*
>
> 3 John 1:2 ESV

Have you heard the old saying, "You can't pour from an empty cup?" What this means is that we must take care of ourselves in order to take care of others. As leaders, nurturers, mothers/fathers, caregivers, helpers or whatever you consider yourself, your wellbeing, health, and self-care matters. **3 John 1:2** ESV says "Beloved, I pray that you may prosper in all things and be in health, just as your soul prospers. Self-care is anything done deliberately to focus on caring for our mental, physical, emotional, and/or spiritual health. **Philippians 4:13** ESV says "I can do all things through Him who strengthens me," meaning we must intentionally take time to be strengthened by Him through His gift of our health. Spiritual self-care involves renewing our minds, guarding our hearts, protecting our bodies like temples, and tending to our spirits. Always remember, self-care starts with Jesus. Serving and caring for yourself is a form of caring for others, which is also self-care. Walking in your purpose is self-care and being good stewards of the gifts and blessings of our minds, bodies, and souls are all self-care.

Self-care is not selfish! Plan a "Me Time" hour(s) or day. What will you do for *YOU* during this time?

REFLECTION:

____

____

____

____

____

____

____

Wakeitha Cunningham is a passion pursuer coach, international best-selling author, speaker, a mother of two, and an influential woman of God on a mission to be a light to God's people. She has a passion for helping others pursue their passions and walk in their God given purpose. Wakeitha encourages others to focus on their passions instead of their problems and pain.

Email: coachwcunningham@gmail.com

SHABBAT SHALOM

Melissa Baines

"There remains, then, a Sabbath-rest for the people of God"

Hebrews 4:9-11 (NIV).

During prayer and meditation one morning, I clearly heard The Lord say, "Hebrews 4:9."

Hebrews 4:9-11 (NIV)

"There remains, then, a Sabbath-rest for the people of God; for anyone who enters God's rest also rests from their works, just as God did from His. Therefore, let us make every effort to enter that rest, so no one will perish by following their example of disobedience."

What I didn't realize was that SHABBAT would begin at 6pm that very same evening and would end the next day at 6pm! Shabbat is Hebrew for the Sabbath, and shalom means peace. It is a common greeting on Friday evenings or throughout the day, until evening on the Sabbath, ultimately wishing someone peace on the Sabbath or wishing them the peace that the Sabbath brings, if you observe it.

Friend, enter into the rest of the Lord!

REFLECTION:

Melissa, more familiarly known as Missy/Sis. Missy, considers herself as one The Lord is completing His Good Work in. Among her many Kingdom Assignments, her most meaningful and heartwarming are that of an adoptive and God mother, missionary, and exhorter. The Lord uses Missy strategically in diverse relationships and networking, where her faith is shared freely.

Social Media FB | Melissa (Missy) Baines

DEVELOP STREAMS OF INCOME

Dr. Derashay Zorn, Kingdom Strategist

"Then the Lord God took the man and put him in the garden of Eden to] tend and keep it."

Gen. 2:15 NKJV

Your purpose, which is known as your message, is to solve a problem within the earth. It is to set you up to have prosperous streams flowing like the garden of Eden. God placed Adam within the garden to work and tend to it. Subsequently, has He placed a purpose in us that is like that garden that we need to work and tend to its business? When we make an effort to move within our purpose, I am confident streams of income will flow from it, just like the streams of living water that flow from our belly. God expects for us to be fruitful and multiply what every He has given unto us. Like the good servant in Luke chapter 19, he got his talent and multiplied it 10 times because he knew how to work his garden of Eden (talent/purpose/message).

God has surely given everyone a message. We hold the responsibility of developing fruitful streams that multiply with it. Discover ways on how you can package it to develop those multiple income streams. You can develop a speaking, professional services, membership, and educational platform for your one message, just to name a few. So, be a good steward of what God has given you. Don't hide your talents and begin to build those income streams.

Dear God, thank you for a message that will develop multiple streams of income within my home, in Jesus' name, amen.

REFLECTION:

____

____

____

____

____

____

Kingdom Strategist, Blueprint Builder, and Spiritual Midwife, Dr. Derashay Zorn is an international business coach and best-selling author. She helps the faith-based community magnetize and monetize their influence and impact by creating profitable brands that develop long-lasting relationships with products and services their ideal client loves.

Discover how she can take your message and develop your next book, membership program, course, educational platform, coaching program, and more by visiting https://px.fyi/teawiththestrategist.

Social Media FB | IG: kingdom.strategist **Website:** www.derashay.com

CONTACT DR. DERASHAY ZORN

FOR BOOKINGS

www.derashay.com or info@derashay.com

AVAILABLE TITLES

IF YOU ENJOYED THIS BOOK, HERE ARE OTHER DR. ZORN BOOKS AVAILABLE ON AMAZON:

Abortions In The Church: Divine Strategies to Spiritual Deliverance Book

Abortions In The Church: Divine Strategies to Spiritual Deliverance Workbook

Meant for My Good: Being Developed in the Midst of the Disaster Anthology

Parentpreneur Success Guide – Co-Author Edition

31 Ways of Influence Volume 1

31 Ways of Influence Volume 2

UPCOMING PROJECTS

Beyond The Vision: Delivering My Expectations

The Rules of Success

ANTHOLOGIES

40: The Wilderness Experience Survival Guide – Entrepreneurship Edition Anthology

I AM H.E.R. Collective Series Anthology

Meant for My Good Anthology V2

31 Ways of Influence V3 Anthology

Join the Next Anthology by visiting https://pxi.fyi/imnextdrzorn

Made in the USA
Columbia, SC
09 February 2022

55829647R00067